KEN KERN'S HOMESTEAD WORKSHOP

KEN KERN'S HOMESTEAD WORKSHOP

BARBARA and KEN KERN

Illustrations by Jim Schmalzried

CHARLES SCRIBNER'S SONS
New York

First Charles Scribner's Sons Paperback Edition 1983

Copyright © 1981 Barbara and Ken Kern

Library of Congress Cataloging in Publication Data

Kern, Barbara.
  Ken Kern's homestead workshop.

  Includes index.
  1. Workshops. I. Kern, Ken, 1927–
II. Title. III. Title: Homestead workshop.
TT152.K47   670.42   81-9378
ISBN 0-684-17846-X   AACR2

1 3 5 7 9 11 13 15 17 19 Q/P 20 18 16 14 12 10 8 6 4 2

Printed in the United States of America.

CONTENTS

By Ken Kern

The Owner-Built Home

The Owner-Built Homestead: A How-to-Do-It Book
  (with Barbara Kern)

Fireplaces: The Owner-Builder's Guide
  (with Steve Magers)

The Owner-Builder and the Code: Politics of Building Your Home
  (with Rob Thallon and Ted Kogon)

Stone Masonry: Owner-Builder's Guide
  (with Steve Magers and Lou Penfield)

The Owner-Built Pole Frame House
  (with Barbara Kern)

Ken Kern's Homestead Workshop
  (with Barbara Kern)

The Work Book: Personal Politics of Building Your Home
  (with Evelyn Turner)

The Healthy House

PART I
THE TOOLS

Man is a tool-using animal.
Without tools he is nothing.
With tools he is all.
Thomas Carlyle, 1832

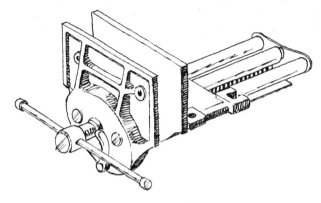

WOODWORKER'S VISE

Figure 1.

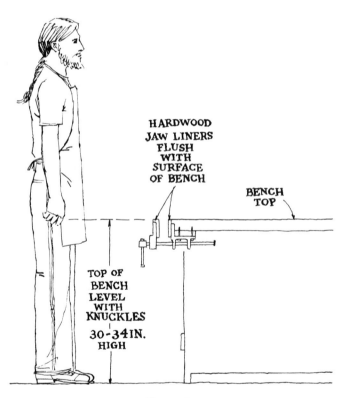

HARDWOOD
JAW LINERS
FLUSH
WITH
SURFACE
OF BENCH

BENCH
TOP

TOP OF
BENCH
LEVEL
WITH
KNUCKLES
30-34 IN.
HIGH

Figure 2.

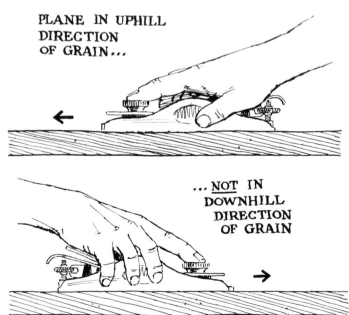

PLANE IN UPHILL
DIRECTION
OF GRAIN...

... NOT IN
DOWNHILL
DIRECTION
OF GRAIN

Figure 3.

Chapter 1
USE OF HAND TOOLS

This is a book about using tools to produce and maintain all manner of useful objects for operating a homestead. Our intention in this section is to show how materials may be "brought to life" through skillful application of hand tools. When proper regard for the tools, materials, and skills used in shopwork is made manifest, homesteaders should experience deep satisfaction with articles they create or repair.

Commonly, would-be homesteaders have learned to use their heads more often than their hands, acquiring manual facility by trial and error, or as a carpenter friend of ours ruefully says, by the cut-and-try method. To become a successful practitioner of shopwork, one must develop the skill to use one's hands as well as one's mental processes.

As an example of attaining proficiency in the use of shop tools, we have chosen the practice of planing wood as an appropriate illustration. The device used for this task is a plane, which is a carpenter's tool for leveling, smoothing, or removing wood. It consists of a smooth or groove-soled stock with an aperture through which a piece of edged steel, or a chisel, passes obliquely.

To plane the surface of a board, it must first be fastened to a workbench with another tool, a vise (illustrated in Figure 1). Both the bench and the vise must be firmly anchored to the shop wall and floor to prevent the slightest wobbling. Unlike a metalworking vise, which is secured to the top of a bench, the wood-worker's vise is fastened to the underside of the workbench. The jaws of the vise are positioned parallel to the outer edge of the bench (Fig. 2), flush with its top surface—an arrangement that accommodates the planing of long boards and, at the same time, frees the countertop for other projects. Similarly, a wide board may be anchored at its optimum work height. Wooden plates attached to the jaws of the vise protect wood material held in their grip.

There is an initial stage in the work process in which the shopworker should try to identify with the material to be shaped and the tool that will shape it. Not only should the straightness of the board and the direction of its grain be visually scrutinized, but the worker should try to understand what will happen when the chisel-like blade of the plane begins to sever wood fibers. If the blade is pushed into or against the wood's grain, fibers will resist the thrust, and the cut of the blade will be jagged, uneven, and splintery. But when the blade is properly applied in the direction of the grain (Fig. 3), there is a free-flowing, even removal of wood. Planing against the grain requires extra physical exertion on the part of the worker (as when one uses dull or inappropriate tools), causing planing strokes to become less accurate. Craftsmanship is nothing more than *control* of both material and tools; when energy is focused solely to operate a tool, control is sacrificed.

Essentially, a plane is a chisel mounted in a metal carrier, a conveyance that necessitates the

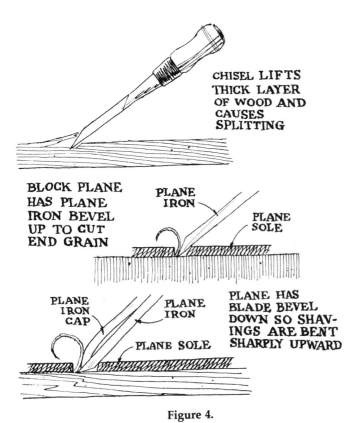

CHISEL LIFTS THICK LAYER OF WOOD AND CAUSES SPLITTING

BLOCK PLANE HAS PLANE IRON BEVEL UP TO CUT END GRAIN

PLANE IRON

PLANE SOLE

PLANE IRON CAP

PLANE IRON

PLANE SOLE

PLANE HAS BLADE BEVEL DOWN SO SHAVINGS ARE BENT SHARPLY UPWARD

Figure 4.

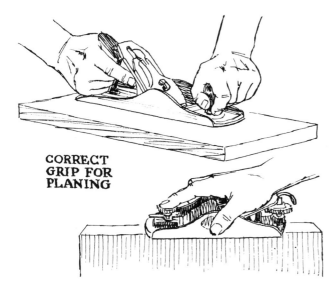

CORRECT GRIP FOR PLANING

Figure 5.

use of both hands to control the depth of cutting (Fig. 4). As shavings peel thinly from the wood, the worker should project him- or herself into the mechanics of use for this tool as well. A wood plane should be thought of as an extension of one's hands, fingernails likened to the cutting surface of the blade as it glides into the butterlike consistency of the material being shaven. This association is important to the proper use of the tool, a concept essential to its skillful manipulation. When the tool is thought of as an extension of self, a worker tends to grasp it with a sense of personal involvement, care, and consideration. The two middle fingers of a worker's hand provide the strength to grasp the tool, and the index finger guides it across the material (Fig. 5). The little finger either curls outward or is tucked out of the way, unneeded in most work processes.

Body stance or bearing influences either a skillful, satisfactory performance or less-than-satisfactory accomplishment resulting in fatigue. The body guides the hand in much the same way that the index finger guides the plane. As a planing stroke is begun, body weight, balanced on the right leg, is placed directly behind the work. As the plane is thrust forward, the body weight moves forward over the work and balance is shifted to the left (Fig. 6). With a plane guided by a knob located on the top of the tool, the left hand pushes downward on the knob while the right hand grips the handle of the plane and guides the tool forward over the surface of the work. Nearing completion of the stroke, weight is transferred again to the right hand while pressure on the left hand is eased upward, preventing one's rounding the end of the board (Fig. 7).

Early in the planing process, a craftsperson must decide which of many planes should be used for a specific planing task (Fig. 8). The *jack plane* is used for coarse work; the *smoothing plane* and the *block plane* are used chiefly for final finish work; and the *jointer plane*, longer than the jack plane, is used to obtain very straight edges. The *compass plane*, similar to the smoothing plane, has a convex undersurface with which to form a concave cylindrical surface; the *rabbet plane* and the *fillister plane* are chiefly used for making grooves and sharp corners; and the *plow plane* is used to channel or groove a board's surface (see Fig. 9).

A shop specializing in woodworking will employ mainly the first four tools mentioned above. For general purpose work, however, a homestead shop will use at least the first two. (We have the first three in our shop.) As the name implies, the jack plane is a "Jack-of-all" work tools, generally used to "true-up" or accurately shape a rough-hewn piece of wood. Final surfacing is done with either a smoothing plane or a jointer plane, whereby any irregularities made by the jack plane are refined. The blade of the smoothing plane and the jointer plane is sharpened straight across and set for a finer cut than the jack plane (Fig. 10).

To plane a piece of wood across its grain or to smooth the edges of plywood paneling, a palm-sized *cross-grain block plane* (Fig. 11) may be used. This tool has a single blade, the cutting bevel of which is turned upward rather than

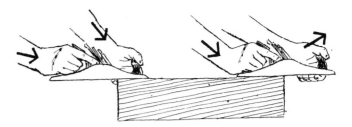

Figure 7.

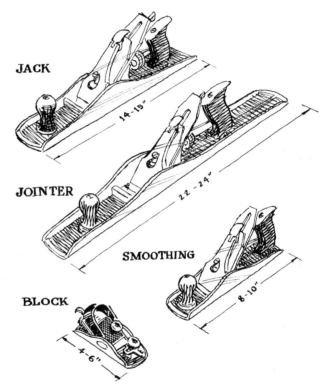

JACK

JOINTER

SMOOTHING

BLOCK

Figure 8.

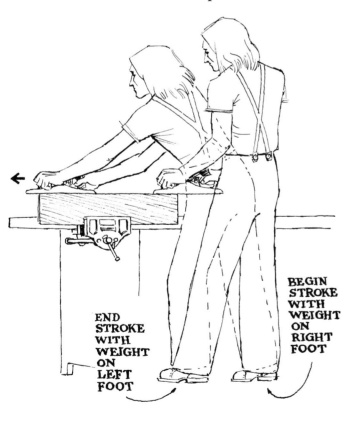

END STROKE WITH WEIGHT ON LEFT FOOT

BEGIN STROKE WITH WEIGHT ON RIGHT FOOT

Figure 6.

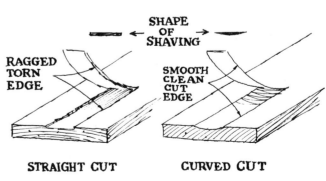

SHAPE OF SHAVING

RAGGED TORN EDGE

SMOOTH CLEAN CUT EDGE

STRAIGHT CUT   CURVED CUT

Figure 9.

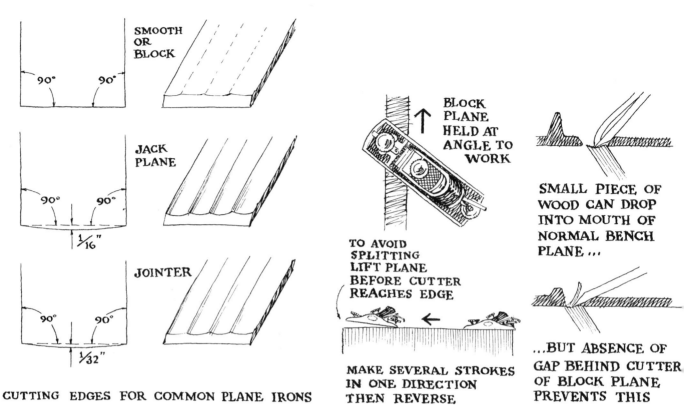

CUTTING EDGES FOR COMMON PLANE IRONS

Figure 10.

Figure 11.

downward, as it is with other types of planes. The angle of the blade, relative to the horizon, is set at 12 degrees for work on hardwood surfaces and at 20 degrees for softwood surfaces. Chips of wood, not shavings, fly from the block plane. Contrary to the way most planes are held, this plane is gripped at an angle to the work (Fig. 12).

Possibly the most frequent error shop owners commit is in making poor choices when purchasing tools. It should be emphatically stated that poor tool selection is less than desirable, even disastrous to wood planing. For example, Stanley Tools makes a cheap line of tools, called Handyman, that is not up to the standards we require. Close inspection reveals rough, unfinished castings and crude, poorly operating adjustments. This company, however, also sells professional-quality tools; their planes in this class are the best in the world. Blades of these planes possess an enduring edge of chrome-cadmium steel, one that, while planing, is easily adjusted for depth of cut by simply flicking a brass nut with the index finger. Handles of

these tools are not cast in plastic, as are those in the cheaper line of tools, but are made of wood. Castings are carefully made and finely finished, and all components fit snugly together and operate with ease.

Understandably, a homesteader might become annoyed with the myriad details involved, for instance, in the task of planing wood: the necessity to learn the various skills, to accumulate appropriate tools, to devote adequate time to the operation. Who needs planed wood anyway? some are thus inclined to ask. For them, "rough-hewn" or "rough-cut" materials are entirely adequate. On the other hand, there are those who value planed-wood surfacing but prefer not to do the work by hand. For them it will be necessary to invest in a portable power plane. This tool requires little skill to operate, is fast, and will turn out professional-quality work. Quality wood planing *is* possible without having to learn to work wood by hand. Ultimately, if one wants quality production in woodworking, investment in power tools is essential.

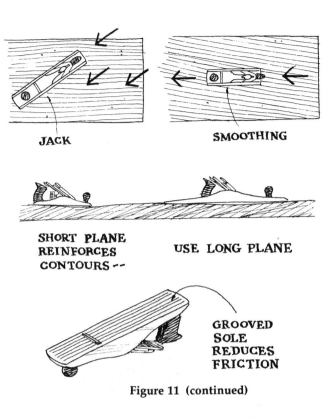

JACK

SMOOTHING

SHORT PLANE
REINFORCES
CONTOURS --

USE LONG PLANE

GROOVED
SOLE
REDUCES
FRICTION

Figure 11 (continued)

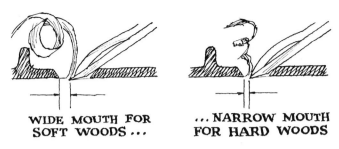

WIDE MOUTH FOR
SOFT WOODS ...

... NARROW MOUTH
FOR HARD WOODS

Figure 12.

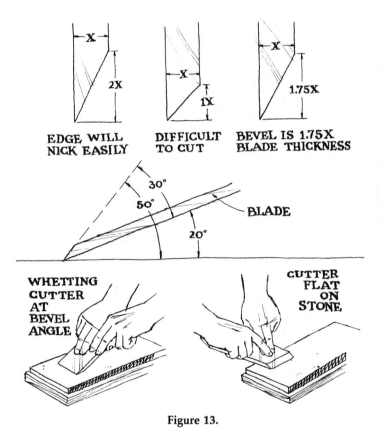

EDGE WILL
NICK EASILY

DIFFICULT
TO CUT

BEVEL IS 1.75X
BLADE THICKNESS

WHETTING
CUTTER
AT
BEVEL
ANGLE

CUTTER
FLAT
ON
STONE

Figure 13.

We should emphasize that the degree of tool proficiency we advocate is *not* that which is requisite to craftsmanship work. Homesteaders' primary need is to make products essential to homestead operation, those used to maintain and repair homestead facilities. Shopwork is thus more a practical than an avocational enterprise. Generally, we plane wood to shape it or prevent its splintering, not merely to achieve slick surfaces. In this book, we are dealing with information for practical usage of tools.

One final matter remains for consideration: tool care and management. Tools must be kept sharp and readily accessible to the area of their use. All of our wood-shaping tools, including a drawknife and several hatchets, are stored in a drawer beneath the woodworking bench. Only sharpened, clean, and lubricated tools are returned to their appointed location. A grinding wheel, whetstone, and oil can are kept within easy reach, facilitating tool maintenance.

In this simple account illustrating wood planing, we have talked about one particular aspect of tool use. In the woodworking and metalworking sections of our homestead shop, there are other divisions of application. These additional categories involve tools that hold, guide, cut, shape, drill, fasten, and sharpen. How tools are employed in each of these basic use-categories is the subject of Part I of this book. Later, we will elaborate on the proper selection, maintenance, and storage locations for tools.

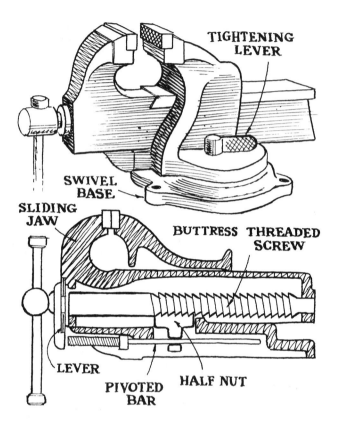

TIGHTENING LEVER

SWIVEL BASE

SLIDING JAW

BUTTRESS THREADED SCREW

LEVER

PIVOTED BAR

HALF NUT

PARALLEL JAW MACHINIST'S VISE

Figure 14.

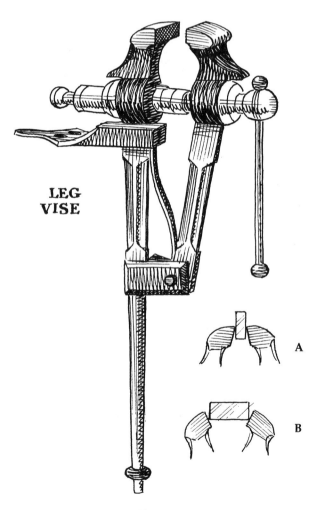

LEG VISE

A

B

Figure 15.

Chapter 2
TOOLS THAT HOLD

There are two kinds of holding tools: those that support and those that grip. A sawhorse or a workbench *supports* material, while a vise or a pair of pliers *grips* material when it is worked. Both kinds of holding tools must meet certain criteria for maximum efficient use.

In our shop, we have devised a multipurpose movable bench, a substitute for the traditional carpenter's sawhorse. It is 4 feet long, 2 feet wide, and 2 feet high; each of its four legs bears 4-inch hard-rubber casters, enabling it to be easily rolled to any part of the shop. When working on engines, it is a handy place to set automotive parts and tools to be cleaned, sorted, or organized. This portable bench can also hold projects that are heavy and awkward. It is the proper height for cutting boards and assembling pieces.

Other benches in the workshop should have no movement; it is essential that they be securely fastened to the shop wall and floor. For woodworking, one bench holds a vise and another bench works in conjunction with a radial arm saw. For metalwork, one bench holds a machinist's vise, grinder, and drill press, while another is used for welding and pipefitting. There are also a paint bench and an automotive maintenance bench.

Both the metalworking and woodworking benches are built of 2-inch-thick rough-sawn lumber. Height is an important design factor. Generally, when one stands erect with arms bent, the elbows should be level with the top of the vise.

For the same reason that it is imperative to securely anchor a bench to the workshop structure, it is also essential to anchor a vise to its bench. Fine bench work cannot be accomplished when there is "play" or "wobble" in either bench or vise; nothing can be more aggravating, frustrating, or unsafe for the serious shopworker.

The biggest advance in the three-thousand-year history of holding-tool design occurred this century with the invention of the parallel jaw (Fig. 14). The leg vise (Fig. 15), which dominated farm workshops earlier this century, is an example of a vise without parallel jaws. The outer jaw of this tool is hinged, and it is impossible for both jaws to meet squarely. Narrow work is gripped between the jaw's upper edges (Fig. 15a), while wider work is gripped between its lower edges (Fig. 15b). Most pliers' design, like that of the common slip joint pliers (Fig. 16), has this same failing. Jaws of the slip joint pliers can be opened wide at the hinge pin to grip work of large diameter, but in either position its holding capacity is negligible because the jaws do not sit squarely on the work. Limited surface contact is made between the pliers and one's work, and invariably the work slips and is scarred. Nothing raises the ire of an experienced shopworker more than the sight of a novice trying to tighten or loosen a nut with a pair of slip joint pliers. Another shoddy design feature of slip joint pliers is the placement of side cutters at the junction of the jaws to make it a combination tool. The homestead craftsper-

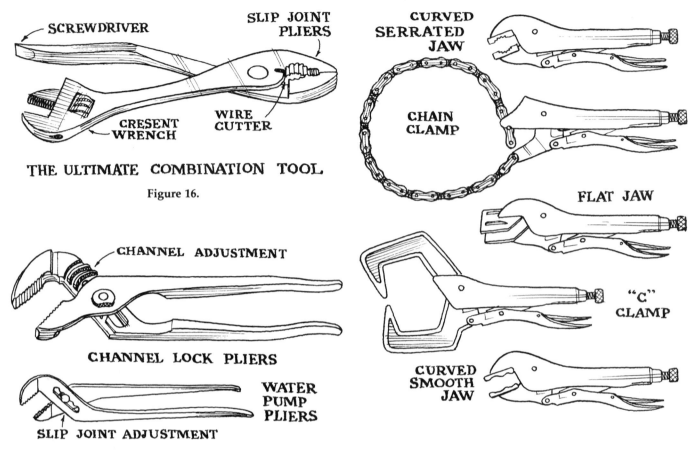

THE ULTIMATE COMBINATION TOOL.

Figure 16.

CHANNEL LOCK PLIERS

SLIP JOINT ADJUSTMENT

Figure 17.

Figure 18. *Types of Vise Grip Pliers*

son should be wary of *any* combination tool, for the original aggregate tool was so ineffectual that the manufacturer added multi-use features to spur its sale. Combination pliers do not cut wire; they "worry" it apart. After a short period of use as a wire cutter, the slip joint pliers become worn and are unable to grip even small objects. When pressure is applied to the handles, jaws of the slip joint may slide apart, a frustration comparable to the turning of the blade of a screwdriver in its wooden handle when pressure is applied to loosen or tighten a screw.

In recent years, three tools—the channel-lock pliers, the vise-grip pliers, and the Bernard parallel-action pliers—have been marketed as improvements over the slip-joint pliers. The channel-lock pliers (Fig. 17) has long handles, insuring a powerful grip on work. It has grooves on one jaw and ridges on the other to give positive (or secure) adjustment where the grooves and ridges match. This design is similar to that of a parallel jaw since there may be six or more positions for adjustment. When shopping for channel lock pliers, do not buy a similar tool, called a water pump pliers (Fig. 17). It, too, opens to six or more positions and has long handles, but work is held by a slip joint, not grooves and ridges. Avoid slip-jointed gripping tools and wooden-handled screwdrivers!

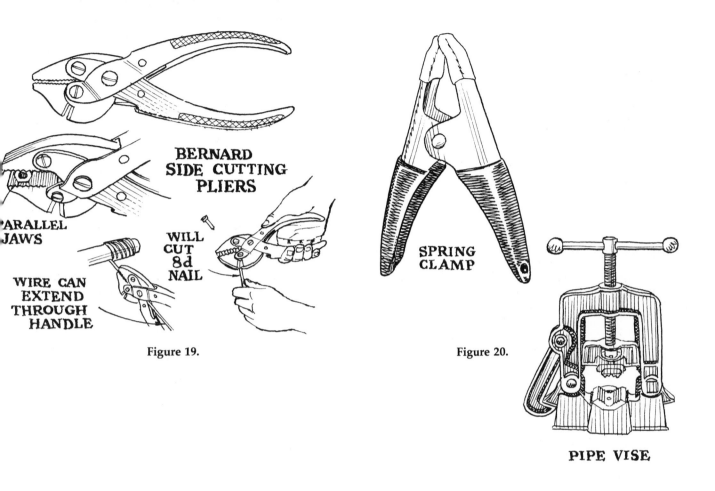

BERNARD
SIDE CUTTING
PLIERS

PARALLEL
JAWS

WIRE CAN
EXTEND
THROUGH
HANDLE

WILL
CUT
8d
NAIL

Figure 19.

SPRING
CLAMP

Figure 20.

PIPE VISE

Another innovation in holding tools has been the invention of the vise grip pliers (Fig. 18), also known as the lever wrench. By turning an adjustment screw at the end of the handle, the pliers are clamped to fit snugly over any size object and then are locked into position. An additional hand lever is activated to release the work. This tool can be used as a clamp or a vise to free one's hands for other functions. In this respect, the vise grip pliers is especially useful in welding work and sheet-metal fabrication.

The Bernard parallel action or side cutting pliers (Fig. 19) also has a viselike grip. Jaws of this tool are flat and wide. Some materials, like wire, may even extend through its handle, out

of the way. As with the vise grip, leverage is compounded in the Bernard pliers, providing great holding power. A unique model has a cutting blade that cuts large nails with ease.

Types of holding tools range from a pair of hand tweezers or spring clamps that require but a few ounces of pressure to operate, to a pipe vise that calls for pressure of a hundred pounds or more (Fig. 20). Incidentally, spring clamps are useful in a wide variety of shop practices; they are one of those tools never missed when not available but often used when around. The best pipe vise is that which has a hinged jaw on one side and a locking device on the other. A screw forces the top jaw through a pair of bot-

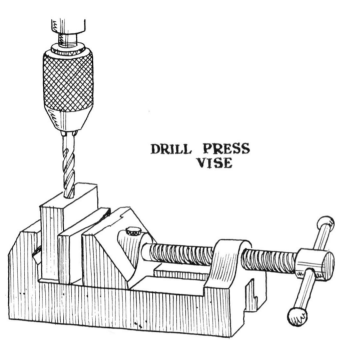

DRILL PRESS VISE

Figure 21.

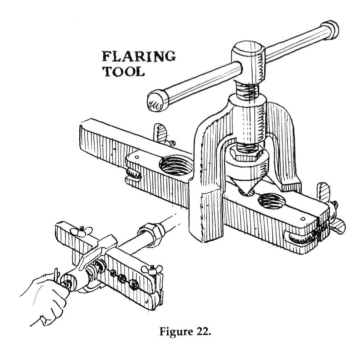

FLARING TOOL

Figure 22.

tom jaws, giving a very positive grip on any round stock or pipe. The chain pipe vise, with only a section of chain to hold work down, cannot begin to compare for holding power with the hinged jaw vise. It is awkward to get an adequate purchase or grip with this chain in order to tighten work in place. Some brands of machinist's bench vises are equipped with auxiliary pipe-holding jaws but these are, for the most part, inadequate to their task. They are like the anvil built at the rear of a vise: one strong blow and the anvil as well as a sizable portion of the cast-iron vise ends up on one's shop floor. Be certain, however, that the machinist's vise you do purchase has a swivel base and a swivel lock on each side.

It is virtually impossible to drill a straight hole in round metal stock without the assistance of a table vise bolted to the bed of a drill press (Fig. 21). This is the sort of seldom-used tool that is, nevertheless, indispensable when needed. It would be a hassle to try to jerry-build a similar holding device, which would never be entirely satisfactory to the task. Another product in the category of essential-but-seldom-used is a flaring tool (Fig. 22). There is no better way to connect tubing of small diameter, yet this tool will seldom be used.

An assortment of bar clamps and C clamps (Fig. 23) should be represented in your homestead workshop. Traditionally, the professionalism of a cabinetmaker was evaluated by the number of handscrew clamps that hung on his shop wall. Today, with quick-setting glues in widespread use, a large number of clamps are not required in a shop; instead of wooden handscrew clamps, we prefer to stock metal C clamps and metal bar clamps that can be used for welding as well. Metalwork requires the use of clamps more often than woodworking processes. A recent improvement in C-clamp assembly is the use of lightweight alloys in place of the malleable iron ordinarily used in the past. The excessive weight of a clamp can be a disadvantage when trying to align pieces of material for their fabrication.

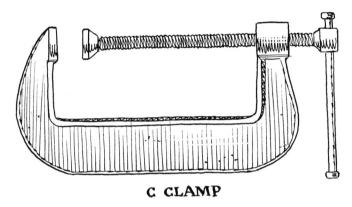

C CLAMP

Figure 23.

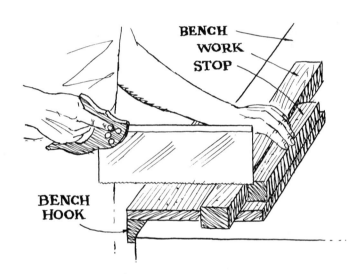

BENCH
WORK
STOP

BENCH
HOOK

Figure 24. *A bench hook, easily constructed from scrap wood, is useful for woodworking projects.*

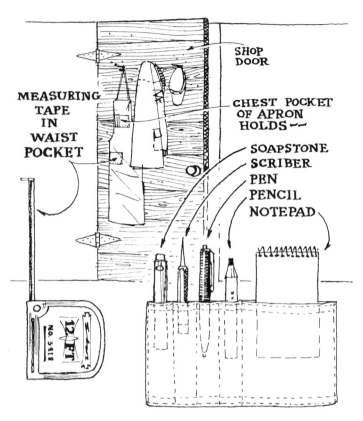

MEASURING TAPE IN WAIST POCKET

SHOP DOOR

CHEST POCKET OF APRON HOLDS ──

SOAPSTONE
SCRIBER
PEN
PENCIL
NOTEPAD

12 FT
NO. 5418

Figure 25.

ANGLE TABLE FOR THE SQUARE

ANGLE	TONGUE	BODY	ANGLE	TONGUE	BODY
1	0.35	20.00	23	7.80	18.40
2	0.70	19.99	24	8.13	18.27
3	1.05	19.97	25	8.45	18.13
4	1.40	19.95	26	8.77	17.98
5	1.74	19.92	27	9.08	17.82
6	2.09	19.89	28	9.39	17.66
7	2.44	19.85	29	9.70	17.49
8	2.78	19.81	30	10.00	17.32
9	3.13	19.75	31	10.28	17.14
10	3.47	19.70	32	10.60	16.96
11	3.82	19.63	33	10.89	16.77
12	4.16	19.56	34	11.18	16.58
13	4.50	19.49	35	11.47	16.38
14	4.84	19.41	36	11.76	16.18
15	5.18	19.32	37	12.04	15.98
16	5.51	19.23	38	12.31	15.76
17	5.85	19.13	39	12.59	15.54
18	6.18	19.02	40	12.87	15.32
19	6.51	18.91	41	13.12	15.09
20	6.84	18.79	42	13.38	14.89
21	7.17	18.67	43	13.64	14.63
22	7.49	18.54	44	13.89	14.39
			45	14.14	14.14

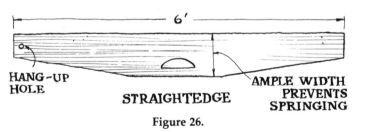

6'

HANG-UP HOLE

STRAIGHTEDGE

AMPLE WIDTH PREVENTS SPRINGING

Figure 26.

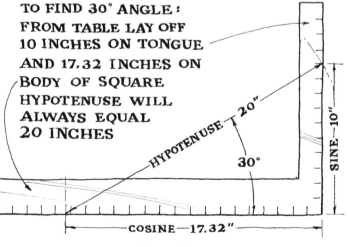

TO FIND 30° ANGLE:
FROM TABLE LAY OFF
10 INCHES ON TONGUE
AND 17.32 INCHES ON
BODY OF SQUARE
HYPOTENUSE WILL
ALWAYS EQUAL
20 INCHES

HYPOTENUSE 20"

30°

SINE 10"

COSINE 17.32"

Figure 27.

Chapter 3
TOOLS THAT GUIDE

Upon entering our homestead workshop, one might notice a cotton work apron hanging from a coat hook screwed to the inside of the entry door. The purpose of the work apron, worn whenever shopwork is done, is to protect clothing and to keep ready for use a few of the shop's most important tools (Fig. 25). In a waist pocket of the apron a 12-foot flex tape is kept handy, and in a chest pocket there are separate pouches for a note pad, a pen, a scriber, a carpenter's pencil, and a soapstone. These "guiding" tools are constantly used for measuring, marking, making notes, or referring to sketches made for the work at hand. It is important to form the habit of wearing an apron containing these implements, for much wasted time and frustration will be averted by having this handful of tools available for immediate use. With them one may measure and mark any kind of wood or metal material. Work may be accurately laid out on a workbench to the closest sixteenth of an inch using the scriber or, on the slab floor of the shop, to the closest half-inch using the soapstone.

Other guiding tools will help with project layout. A 6-foot-long plywood straightedge (Fig. 26) is as indispensable to shopwork as the steel square (also called a carpenter's or framing square) and a chalk line. The concrete floor in the central section of our shop is laid thicker than usual and finished uniformly level and smooth. It is a large flat surface that lends itself to the marking of outlines for a full-sized job. Cement nails, when partially driven into this floor slab, may serve as radius points for curvilinear shapes. While working directly on this surface, using a spirit level and a plumb bob, wooden or metal objects may be built both square and plumb.

The steel square can be used to determine when a member is plumb (or exactly perpendicular to another member) or when it is at a right angle (or squared) with the rest of the work. With one leg on a level surface, its other leg rises exactly vertical. These long legs, one 16 inches and the other 24 inches long, tend to make the steel square more accurate than smaller measuring tools because it can span greater lengths, compensating for irregularities in the material. Entire books have been written about the many uses carpenters have for the steel square, but we use it in the homestead workshop principally for layout work. Because of its large size, the steel square can also determine any angle with an accuracy greater than that of a protractor. Simple trigonometric sine and cosine functions have been mathematically calculated to register any angle from 1 degree to 45 degrees. In the table illustrated (Fig. 27), the hypotenuse is constant—in every case it is 20 inches in length. Once determined, an angle may be conveniently transferred to a sliding T-bevel (Fig. 28), a tool that can be locked in position by tightening a screw lever that is located, preferably, at the end of the stock. This angle can then be marked off on the material to be cut or shaped.

After the flex tape, the guiding tool in most

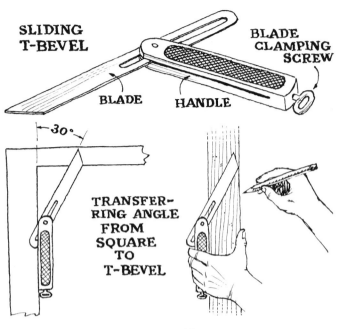

SLIDING T-BEVEL

BLADE CLAMPING SCREW

BLADE   **HANDLE**

30°

TRANSFER-RING ANGLE FROM SQUARE TO T-BEVEL

Figure 28.

common use is a combination square (Fig. 29), without doubt the most successful "combination" tool ever invented. We like it because it combines various single functions, like those of the try square and the marking gauge, and has but one hand-tightened nut to adjust. Thus the blade can be locked in any position, making it useful as a depth gauge. The head is shaped for marking either 90- or 45-degree angles, or it may be removed entirely from its 12-inch rule for use as a straightedge. Most combination squares have built-in vials with which level or plumb is registered. A cavity is found in the handle of some combination squares to hold a short scriber.

Another well-designed guiding tool is the chalk box (Fig. 30). Contemporary shopsmiths and builders tend to take this remarkable tool for granted, but it was only a few years ago that carpenters still marked a straight line by rubbing a hunk of blue chalk along a heavy cotton string. Now we merely pour powdered chalk into an aluminum container that houses string on a reel. After use, as it rewinds into its box, the line is once again coated with chalk. A clip on the loose end of the line may be hooked to the edge of material or over a nail. A string-locking device in the container secures the line

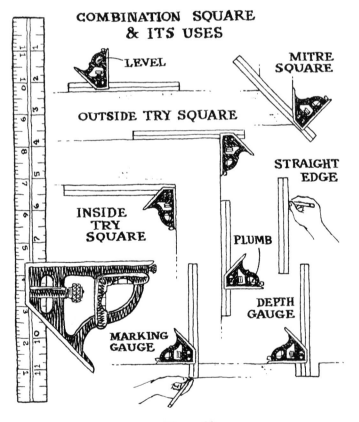

COMBINATION SQUARE & ITS USES

LEVEL

MITRE SQUARE

OUTSIDE TRY SQUARE

STRAIGHT EDGE

INSIDE TRY SQUARE

PLUMB

DEPTH GAUGE

MARKING GAUGE

Figure 29.

HOOK & RING

FOLDING REWIND CRANK

CHALK BOX

Figure 30.

at a fixed position, so that, when the container end is pulled, the line is made taut. This feature also makes it possible to use the chalk box as a rudimentary plumb bob on occasion.

To register a straight chalked line, the string must be pulled up at a right angle to the material beneath it; otherwise, when it is snapped, or released, the resulting mark will curve. The string should be tight enough to leave a straight line when snapped, but not so tight that chalk will fly from the string before it strikes the surface to be marked. The string is always snapped near the end where you are holding it, not from the middle of the line as might be expected. Experienced carpenters assert two general rules for snapping a chalk line: (1) The point of release should be equal in inches to what the overall distance is in feet, and (2) the line should be pulled upward one inch for every three feet of length. For example, as illustrated in Figure 31, to mark an 8-foot panel of plywood from end to end, you should grip the line 8 inches from the end held, pulling it up about 3 inches above the material before releasing it. This procedure will produce a flawless mark on the plywood.

Today, we are fortunate to have nylon line, a thin, twisted braid of tough string that is purported to withstand a pull of up to 150 pounds without breaking. In practice, however, a safe work load for this string is only 20 percent this amount of pull or a breaking strength of 30 pounds. Thin, lightweight, yet able to resist such force, this line can be stretched without appreciable sag. It is possible to affix to this line such handy tools as a line level (as shown in Figure 32), a practice unheard of in the days of heavy cotton line.

On a flat shop floor, a line level or a regular carpenter's level may be used to advantage when working on large layouts. Likewise, a plumb bob is used to both guide and test your calculations and to verify the results of your work. Sighting with a plumb bob, called "eyeballing" (Fig. 33), can be more accurate than using a level, because slight variations in the object being sighted may be averaged—varia-

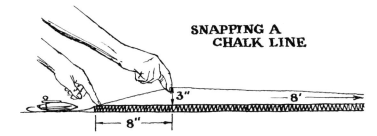

Figure 31.

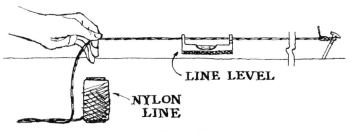

LINE LEVEL

NYLON LINE

Figure 32.

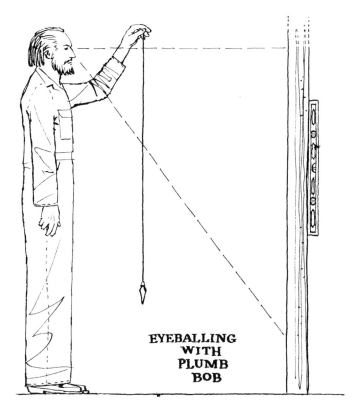

EYEBALLING WITH PLUMB BOB

Figure 33.

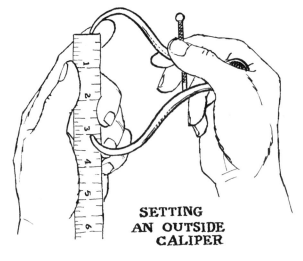

**SETTING
AN OUTSIDE
CALIPER**

Figure 34.

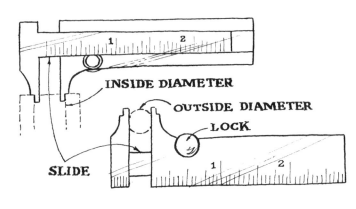

INSIDE DIAMETER

OUTSIDE DIAMETER

LOCK

SLIDE

SLIDE CALIPER

Figure 36.

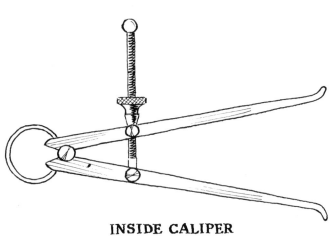

INSIDE CALIPER

Figure 35.

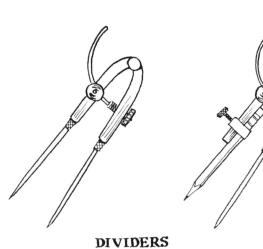

DIVIDERS

Figure 37.

tions that would throw off readings for plumb from a level.

For more accurate measurement, especially when working with metal, there are *four indispensable tools* needed in the homestead workshop. One is an *outside caliper*, which measures outside diameters. As illustrated in Figure 34, this tool is bowlegged and has a spring joint and an adjustment screw. The *inside caliper* (Fig. 35) also has a spring joint and an adjustment screw, but it has straight legs with feet turned outward to measure inside diameters. A single

tool, the *slide caliper* (Fig. 36), performs both inside and outside assessments and gives an exact reading of the measurement, eliminating the need to transfer it to a rule. The slide caliper also has a locking screw, which holds the jaws of the tool in position during use. Finally, a *pair of dividers* (Figs. 37 and 38), equipped with two metal legs, can span and register distance along a straight line. Some brands of this tool have a removable leg, which may be replaced with a pencil so that it doubles as a compass and can be used to lay out an arc or a circle.

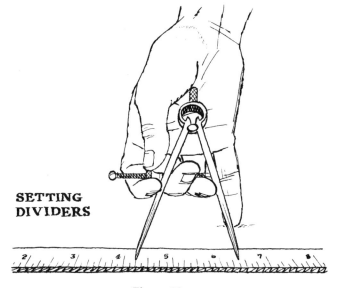

SETTING DIVIDERS

Figure 38.

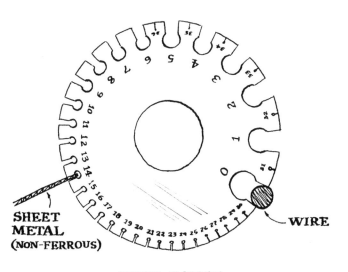

SHEET METAL
(NON-FERROUS)

WIRE

WIRE GAUGE

Figure 39.

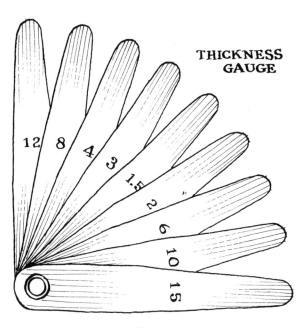

THICKNESS GAUGE

Figure 40.

The definitive descriptive word for all guiding tools is *accuracy*. To achieve a high degree of precision, these tools must be easily adjustable, having a locking mechanism, and be easily read. Adequate illumination is necessary for accurate reading of the tool gauges or indicators. Marking tools must be kept sharp and clean.

A wire gauge (Fig. 39) may be used to measure the diameter of wire or the thickness of nonferrous sheet metal. A tool of similar design is the tap-and-drill gauge. Using this tool, a homestead mechanic can select the correct drill size to accommodate the machine-screw taps used to cut threads. He or she can thus cut a full thread through just the right amount of stock without breaking the tap.

To perform automotive shop tasks, a thickness or "feeler" gauge (Fig. 40) is indispensable. This tool has a number of thin steel leaves, one varying from the next by only thousandths of an inch. The leaves may be used singly or in combination, enabling the mechanic—within the limits of the tool—to create any dimension necessary.

PROPER GRIP
FOR
ACCURATE
CUTS

Figure 41.

CROSSCUT
SET

RIPSAW
SET

CENTER
NOT
CUT

EXCESSIVE
SET

Figure 43.

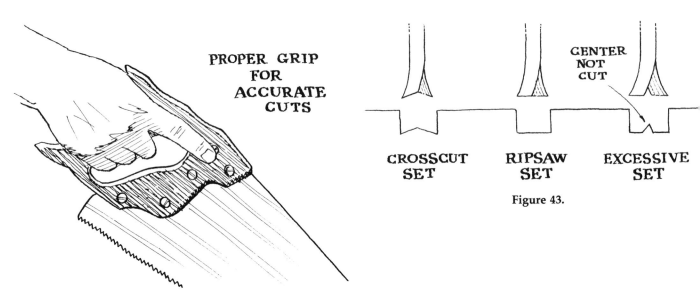

BEGINNING
THE
CUT

Figure 42.

90°

RIP
SAW
TEETH

60°   90°

65°

CROSS
CUT
TEETH

80°

60°

Figure 44.

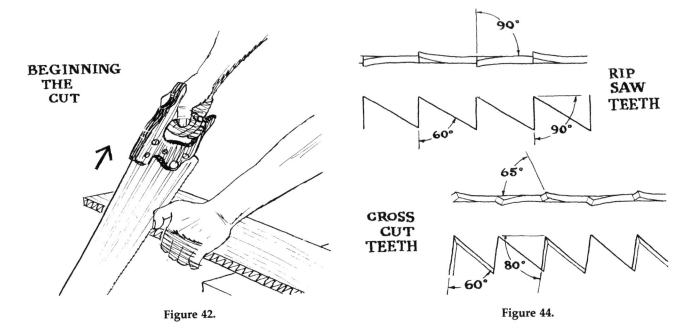

Chapter 4
CUTTING TOOLS

The first hand-operated cutting tools that come readily to mind when beginning to equip a homestead workshop are handsaws for cutting wood and hacksaws for cutting metal (which may also be cut with a chisel or tin snips). The saw is basically a simple tool, a strip of thin metal with teeth along one edge and a wooden handle at one end (Fig. 41). The back of the saw is ground thinner than its toothed edge to reduce friction with the saw cut or kerf. By careful hammering of the blade during manufacture, the metal of the saw blade becomes "tensioned" or flexible while stiff. The technique for tensioning and tapering saw blades is centuries old. In 1677, Joseph Moxon,* an English tool historian, described the process:

But if it bend into a regular bow all the way, and be stiff, the Blade is good: It cannot be too stiff, because they are but Hammer-hardened, and therefore often bow when they fall under unskillful Hands, but never break, unless they have been often bowed in that place. The Edge whereon the Teeth are, is always made thicker than the Back, because the Back follows the Edge, and if the Edge should not make a pretty wide Kerf, if the Back do not strike in the Kerf, yet by never so little irregular bearing, or twisting of the Hand awry, it must so stop, as to bow the SAW; and (as I said before) with often bowing it will break at last.

*Joseph Moxon, *Mechanick Exercises: or the Doctrine of Handy-works, Applied to the Arts of Smithing, Joinery, Carpentry, Turning, Bricklayery* (London, 1677).

The set or adjustment of a saw's teeth is another design factor contributing to free and easy cutting action; teeth are bent in alternate directions away from the blade so that the saw cut, or kerf, is wider than the thickness of the blade. With taper-ground saw blades, a greater angle of set is not so critical as one without taper. Quality saws also become narrower from handle to tip, the tip being thinner. As illustrated in Figure 43, less set means a smoother cut. If the set of a saw blade is too great, center portions of the kerf will not be fully cut. Two-way taper-ground blades are also more flexible and provide better balance and heft.

There are different configurations of saw teeth for cutting wood *across* the grain (crosscutting) or *with* the grain (rip cutting). When cutting with the grain, or along the tree's axis, there is less opportunity for teeth to dig into the wood; therefore, the cutting edge of a ripsaw is customarily set at right angles to the blade of the saw (Fig. 44). Teeth in a ripsaw have a chisellike cutting action. Teeth in a crosscut saw have a greater angle so that they cut out or slice like a knife but do not chisel wood grain. Being bevel filed, the teeth actually shear wood fibers.

The angle that saw teeth make in relation to the blade is critical. If the angle is too pointed, teeth will embed in the wood; if too flat, they glide over the wood (Fig. 45). Sixty degrees is optimal for cutting hardwood, since this angle makes a stronger tooth than the 45-degree angle commonly set for cutting softwoods (Fig. 46).

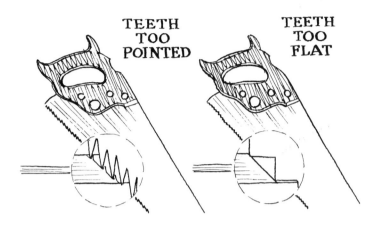

TEETH TOO POINTED   TEETH TOO FLAT

Figure 45.

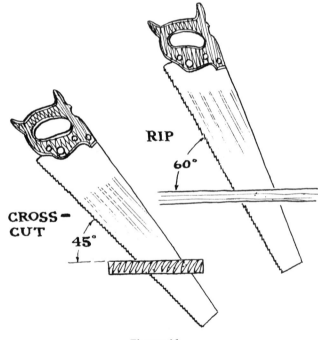

RIP

60°

CROSS-CUT

45°

Figure 46.

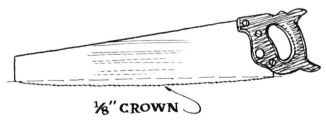

⅛" CROWN

Figure 47.

Quality saws have a slight crown along the tooth edge (as in Figure 47) to make for easier sawing since fewer teeth are then in contact with the wood. This is especially important when ripping wood.

Tooth spacing is also important to the wood-cutting process. The number of teeth per inch determines whether the blade is coarse or fine. A saw with coarse teeth, five per inch, is best used when cutting green wood or when a rapid cut is desired. A fine saw with eight teeth per inch is best used when accurate, smooth cuts are to be made in seasoned wood. Naturally, a saw with fewer teeth will cut faster than one with more teeth per inch. But, in the latter case, accuracy and smoothness are sacrificed for speed. The backsaw, with fourteen teeth per inch, is used primarily in a miter box (Fig. 48) to make either beveled or squared cuts, which must fit with close tolerance. The spline along the top edge of a backsaw is reinforced to stiffen the blade, contributing to its accuracy.

A pistol-grip compass saw will cut curved shapes or circular cutouts. It has a ripsaw tooth pattern and can be started from a half-inch hole. The keyhole saw is simply a finer-toothed compass saw with a narrower blade, so named because it was originally designed to cut keyholes in doors (Fig. 49).

A hacksaw is a bow saw, widely used in the homestead workshop for cutting metals too thick for a tin snips or too thin for a cutting torch. The frame of this saw is adjustable, receiving blades from 8 to 16 inches long. However, as there is seldom any need to make this adjustment, we find the English hacksaw, which can only be adjusted by removing a set screw and which has a single permanent blade length, to be an improvement over the American hacksaw, which collapses every time the tightening screw is released. (See Figure 50.)

Metal-cutting blades are made of tempered high-grade tool steel. Professional machinists purchase those which are hardened throughout the blade, while nonprofessionals will tend to use blades in which only the teeth are hardened—the kind available in tool supply stores. Since the nonprofessional may not know how to use a hacksaw properly, blades with hardened teeth are more flexible and have greater longevity. It is also important to know how to select an appropriate blade, install a blade in a saw frame, and hold the tool properly while material is being sawn.

Metal cutting is done only with the forward stroke of the hacksaw, so its teeth should always point away from you. As each stroke is made, your body should sway ahead and then back with the saw, as it is returned to the start of its stroke. On its return, lift the blade slightly from the surface of the cut and maintain long, slow, steady strokes—about forty per minute. If the cut is made too rapidly, saw teeth become hot and lose their correct temper or strength. Your grip on the hacksaw must be firm, with the index finger pointed forward to guide the saw (Fig. 51). Your free hand holds the front part of the saw, equalizing pressure on the work and helping to guide the blade. (English hacksaws have an improved handle design as well.)

Efficient, high-quality work done with a hacksaw depends as much on your selection of blades as it does on proper use of the saw. This selection is based partly on the fact that three consecutive teeth of the blade should be in contact with the work at all times—as each tooth starts its cut, the two teeth ahead of it will still be cutting (Fig. 52). To start a cut with a hacksaw blade, it may be necessary at times to angle the saw across the work. Also, to preserve the life of the blade, the cut should be started downward, along the surface of the material, as illustrated in Figure 53, not at an edge.

Generally, heavy, even pressure is applied to a coarse-toothed blade to saw thick material; light, steady pressure is applied to a fine-toothed blade to cut thin material. Pressure is light for soft material and heavy for hard material. As listed in Figure 54, a blade with fourteen teeth per inch is used to cut soft steel, aluminum, brass, and copper. Use a blade with eighteen teeth per inch to cut iron pipe and light angle iron and for general shopwork. A twenty-four-toothed blade is used to cut tubing and conduit, sheet steel, and hard materials; thin sheet metal and thin-walled conduit are best cut with a blade that has thirty-two teeth per inch.

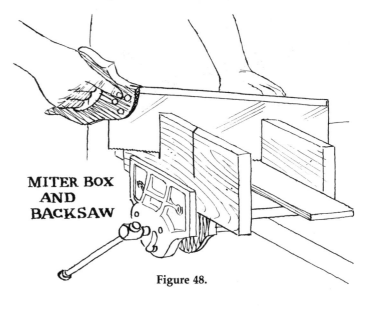

MITER BOX AND BACKSAW

Figure 48.

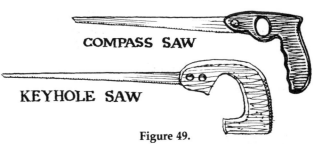

COMPASS SAW

KEYHOLE SAW

Figure 49.

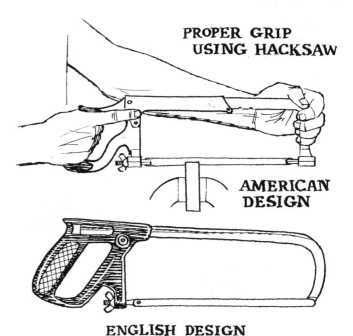

PROPER GRIP USING HACKSAW

AMERICAN DESIGN

ENGLISH DESIGN

Figure 50.

MAKING LONG CUT NEAR EDGE OF MATERIAL

Figure 51.

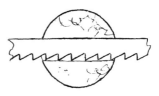

14 TEETH PER INCH FOR LARGE SECTIONS OF MILD MATERIAL

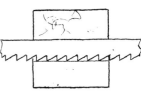

18 TEETH PER INCH FOR LARGE SECTIONS OF TOUGH STEEL

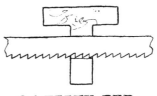

24 TEETH PER INCH FOR ANGLE IRON, HEAVY PIPE BRASS, COPPER

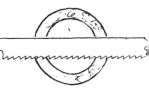

32 TEETH PER INCH FOR THIN TUBING

Figure 54.

INCORRECT

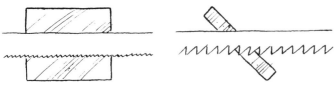

TEETH CLOG

TEETH STRADDLE MATERIAL

CORRECT

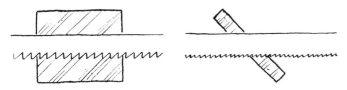

AMPLE CHIP CLEARANCE

THREE OR MORE TEETH ON MATERIAL

Figure 52.

WAVE SET ~ FOR CUTTING THIN STOCK

RAKER SET ~ FOR CUTTING MATERIAL OF UNIFORM SIZE

Figure 55.

INCORRECT

CORRECT

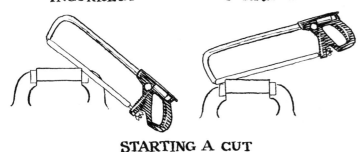

STARTING A CUT

Figure 53.

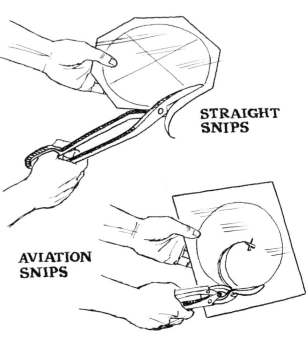

STRAIGHT SNIPS

AVIATION SNIPS

Figure 56.

Blades designed to cut thin stock have teeth set in groups, or waves, so that there is less strain on individual teeth. The teeth of other blades are arranged similarly to those of wood saw blades except that every third tooth is not *set*. This tooth is called a raker tooth, for its function is to clean out the saw kerf (Fig. 55).

Except when sectioning tubing, it is more practical to use a tin snips to cut thin metal. Several types of snips are available (Fig. 56): those used to cut a straight line or those that will cut a curve from stock of up to 20-gauge thickness. Regular, so-called straight snips are used to cut straight lines or circles of large diameter; they are available in models designed for either right-handed or left-handed persons.

One contribution to tool advancement came from the World War II aircraft industry. Aviation snips were designed to cut heat-treated aluminum alloys and stainless steel. Although they have shorter handles than regular snips, aviation snips provide greater leverage in cutting stock of up to 50-gauge. The cutting edge of their blades is equipped with small serrations, which prevent the snips from slipping backward when a cut is made.

To cut sheet metal, place the material flat on a workbench and hold the snips with the flat sides of the blades at right angles to the surface of the work (Fig. 57). This avoids edges that will otherwise be somewhat bent and burred. The resulting piece of scrap will be forced downward by the cutting action of the snips so that it will not interfere with the cutting process. Use the rear portion of the blade for leverage to cut heavy material and prevent the springing, or distortion, of the blades.

Some cutting tools, such as the utility knife (Fig. 58), are merely sharp-edged, not toothed. This particular tool has a reversible, replaceable blade that may be changed by removing a screw in its handle to expose a cache of spare, sharp blades.

Another useful sharp-edged cutting tool is the chisel, made either for cutting wood (a wood chisel) or metal (a cold chisel). Both are essential for a well-equipped homestead workshop. There are three types of wood chisels that are classified by their handle (Fig. 59): that with

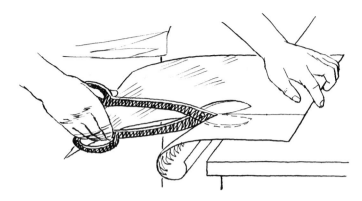

Figure 57.

UTILITY KNIFE

Figure 58.

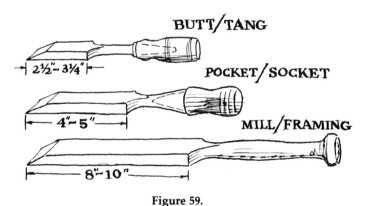

BUTT/TANG

POCKET/SOCKET

MILL/FRAMING

2½"–3¼"

4"–5"

8"–10"

Figure 59.

PARING

Figure 60.

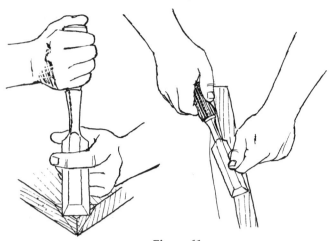

Figure 61.

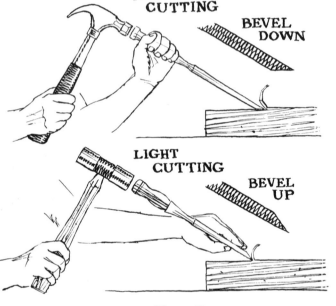

HEAVY CUTTING

BEVEL DOWN

LIGHT CUTTING

BEVEL UP

Figure 62.

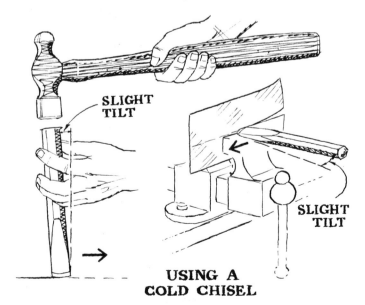

SLIGHT TILT

SLIGHT TILT

USING A COLD CHISEL

Figure 63.

a tang handle is worked by hand pressure and is called a *paring chisel* (Figs. 60 and 61). The chisel with a socket handle, called a *firmer chisel*, is worked with a mallet, and the heavy-duty handle found on the *framing chisel* is struck with a steel hammer (Fig. 62). Each has a different cutting angle, which is always greater for a chisel worked by hand than one worked by wielding a hammer. Each chisel blade also differs in thickness. Again, lesser thickness is required for the chisel worked by hand than one worked by hammer. Wood chisels are also classified by the length of their blade. The shortest of these is the butt chisel (Fig. 59), so called because of its short blade. It is desirable for close, accurate work, its blade being only 3 inches long. The pocket chisel is up to 5 inches long and the mill chisel is up to 10 inches long. Each is available in 1/8-inch increments, from 1/4 inch to 2 inches wide. The variety of wood chisels available is enormous.

The important thing to remember when working with a wood chisel is to cut *with* the grain of the wood. A single, deep cut is not as productive as a series of shallower cuts. The blade should be in a bevel-down position for rough hammer cutting and bevel-up for fine hand cutting, as shown in Figure 62. The chisel should be slanted slightly, diagonally, in the direction of the cut to produce the shearing or paring action necessary to achieve both end-grain and with-the-grain cuts. With right-handed people, the right hand drives the chisel while the left hand controls the work. Holding the blade firmly with knuckles upward, the left hand presses downward on the blade, regulating the depth and length of the cut.

To hold a cold chisel when cutting metal is another matter. A machinist's hammer is always used to drive this chisel (Fig. 63); the thicker the metal, the larger the chisel and the heavier the hammer should be. A heavy chisel struck with a light hammer will not cut thick material. As illustrated, hold the chisel loosely between your thumb and forefinger and wrap remaining fingers loosely around the shank of the tool. Make sharp, quick blows with the hammer to drive the chisel along. A slight angle is maintained between the material and the tool so that the chisel will move gradually ahead, away from you.

If the cutting angle is too slight when hard metal is cut, the cold chisel will soon be dulled. If the angle is too great, excessive force will be required to drive home the blade. Therefore, to hew hard thick metal use a chisel with a 70-degree cutting bevel. Soft metals are best cut with chisels that have an angle or bevel of from 40 to 60 degrees (Fig. 64). The cutting edge of the chisel should be slightly curved to prevent its corners from grooving the surface of your work. To remove or gouge metal, the cutting edge of the bevel of a chisel should be held parallel to the surface of the work.

A solid punch may be used to make a hole in metal, or a center punch may be used to start a hole for a drill bit (Fig. 65). The two differ in how fine their point is ground. A third type, the pin punch, is used to drive out or remove pins. Invariably, it is best to start pins with a solid punch, the stronger tool. The pin punch is used only when the diameter of the pin hole exceeds that of the solid punch. As its name suggests, the prick punch is used to make a very small opening or puncture in the metal.

The art of cutting threads for nuts and bolts is a shop craft that originated during the Middle Ages. A famous illustration done by Leonardo da Vinci shows a three-sectional metal-cutting tap then used to cut the threads of a die which, in turn, threaded a wooden cylinder. This die, called a screw box, is still used to form threads in wood, and it is illustrated in Figure 66. Formerly, wooden threads were used to make many hand tools, such as clamps and marking gauges.

Today, the homesteader will encounter two types of threads: those penetrating a nut or a piece of metal are called "female" threads; those found externally on the shaft of a bolt, rod, or pipe are commonly called "male" threads. Virtually every shop project and certainly any maintenance program will require that the homesteader be able to cut metal threads. Tools used to cut female threads are called taps and those used to cut male threads are called dies.

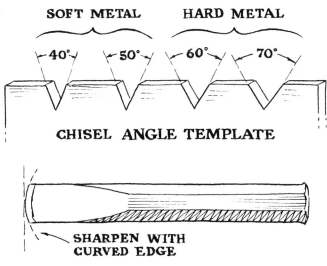

SOFT METAL   HARD METAL

40°   50°   60°   70°

CHISEL ANGLE TEMPLATE

SHARPEN WITH CURVED EDGE

Figure 64.

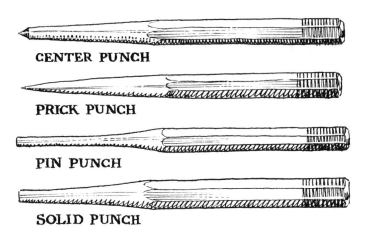

CENTER PUNCH

PRICK PUNCH

PIN PUNCH

SOLID PUNCH

Figure 65.

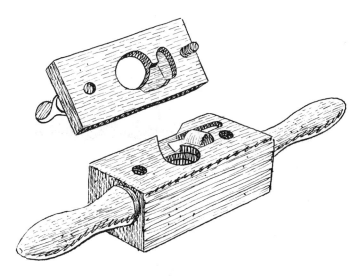

DA VINCI SCREW BOX

Figure 66.

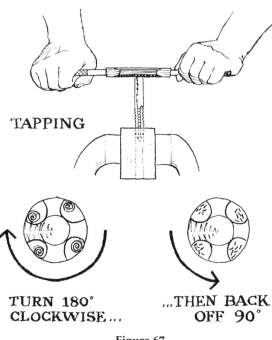

TAPPING

TURN 180°
CLOCKWISE...

...THEN BACK
OFF 90°

Figure 67.

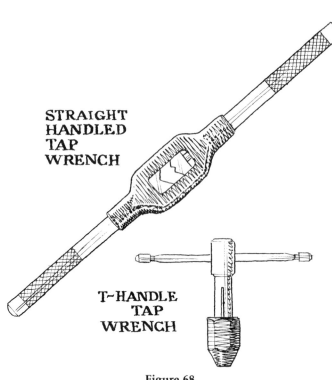

STRAIGHT
HANDLED
TAP
WRENCH

T-HANDLE
TAP
WRENCH

Figure 68.

Threads that are coarse are called National Coarse (NC) and those that are fine are called National Fine (NF). Pipe threads are classified differently, for they are tapered to provide an airtight and liquidtight seal. In a foot of thread, the taper will be 3/4 inch or 1/16 inch for each inch of run or length.

Generally, internal female taps are seldom employed in homestead shopwork, but external dies are used with frequency. To cut male threads, it is important to lubricate metal surfaces with liberal amounts of special "cutting" oil. Before commercially prepared cutting oils became available, machinists concocted their own half-and-half mixture of white lead and lard oil, which was applied to the cutting sur-

face with a small brush. Tallow was also commonly used. To cut copper or aluminum, it is advisable to use a much lighter lubricant, like turpentine. Brass and cast iron are cut dry.

The cutting die must be firmly pressed against the pipe, rod, or bolt to start cutting action, as shown in Figure 67. It will then self-feed as the die is turned clockwise 180 degrees. When the face of the die is flush with the end of the pipe, it can be reversed and removed.

To thread a solid metal rod requires choosing between fine or coarse threads, for the diameter of the rod determines the size of the die that must be used. First, a slight chamfer or angular surface is ground onto the rod, removing its sharp edge so that threads may be properly

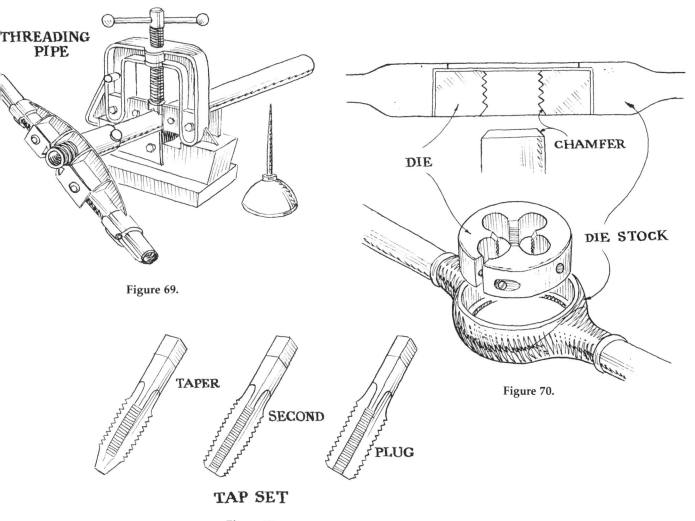

THREADING PIPE

Figure 69.

DIE

CHAMFER

DIE STOCK

Figure 70.

TAPER

SECOND

PLUG

TAP SET

Figure 71.

aligned. Cutting teeth of the die are also chamfered or angled. To cut threads evenly, the rod must be clamped in a vise in a vertical position. Both hands on the diestock help to exert equal pressure downward against the rod while the handles of the wrench are turned clockwise. After the die has begun to cut, back off or reverse a quarter of a turn for each half turn made forward in order to break and remove metal chips formed in the cutting process.

Critical to tap or die cutting is matching the size of the material to the size of the tap or die. As a general rule, there should be a 75 percent difference between the diameter of the hole and the thread to be cut. If the thread is greater than 75 percent of the stock, weak, shallow threads

will result. If the thread is less than 75 percent of the stock, clearance will be obstructed and threads will be cut with difficulty and be ragged. It is also likely that the tap or die will be broken as a result. Refer to the chart on page 147 to determine the drill size to use in producing a given thread size.

One way to prevent a tap from breaking is to start threads with a taper. Once started, a second tap can be used. To reach the bottom of a tapered or blind hole, a third tap is used. Called a bottoming or plug tap, it has full-sized threads to its tip.

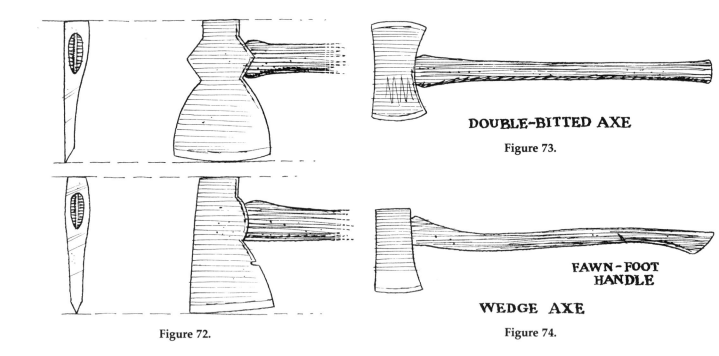

DOUBLE-BITTED AXE

Figure 73.

FAWN-FOOT HANDLE

WEDGE AXE

Figure 74.

Figure 72.

USING A WEDGE AXE

Figure 75.

Chapter 5
TOOLS THAT SHAPE

Once material is cut to an approximate size, it often must be shaped further prior to finishing (such as sanding or painting). We have separated shaping tools into two categories: those for the rough working and those for the smooth working of materials.

To work or shape wood, the primary rough-shaping tool is the axe. This most useful device is also the most ancient of tools. Axe design as we know it today has changed little since medieval times. The head of the broad axe, for example, is now less broad but still used to hew timber, to "square" it or give it flat sides. Even now this axe-head design is forged with a symmetrical shape and a single beveled blade so that it may be reversed for use by left-handed persons (Fig. 72).

The chief advance in axe design occurred during the Bronze Age when a metal forger learned to cast an axe head with a hole into which a handle could be inserted. Before that time, the handle was split to receive the axe head, which was bound to a handle with a thong. The Romans perfected an axe-head design that had a tapered eye or shaft opening for the handle and a hammer-head butt. The last major improvement in axe design happened in this country during the mid-nineteenth century when a "fawn-foot" handle (see Figure 74) was added to the felling axe. As this tool is swung, the woodsman retains a fixed grip with one hand at the end of the handle while the other hand is free to slide toward the head of the axe when it is raised aloft or toward the other hand for the working or downward stroke.

Yankee ingenuity is also responsible for contriving the double-bitted axe (Fig. 73), once called the Methodist axe by irreverent pioneers because it was "two-faced." The original purpose of this design was to reserve one side of the blade for limbing and grubbing, while preserving the other "cleaner," or sharper, edge for felling timber.

Other American axe designs include the familiar wedge axe (Fig. 74), about which British tool historian W. L. Goodman remarks, "It is curious to reflect that this, the final product of 6000 years of incessant trial and experiment, is perhaps the simplest and most functional of all."[*] The outstanding characteristics of this axe were its weight, proportions, and swollen wedgelike blade. For the first time in the history of axe making, the blade-end of the head was made lighter than the butt-end. This important aerodynamic feature allowed the woodsman to deliver a steadier, more forceful and precise blow (Fig. 75). Too, its thick-but-tapered blade was easier to retrieve from wood. To this day, this axe is used to split wood.

In the workshop, to rough-shape a piece of wood, a hatchet is often used more than an axe. A wide variety of hatchets are made. One tool catalogue lists nine types: the broad, half, claw, flooring, shingling, box, car-building, trades-

[*]W. L. Goodman, *A History of Woodworking Tools* (London: Bell, 1964).

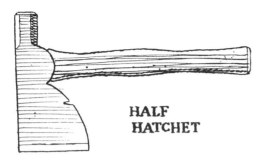

HALF HATCHET

Figure 76.

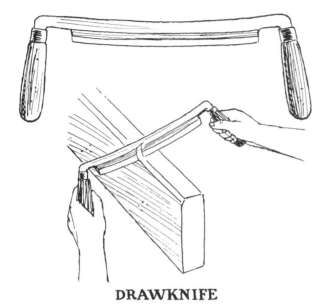

DRAWKNIFE

Figure 77.

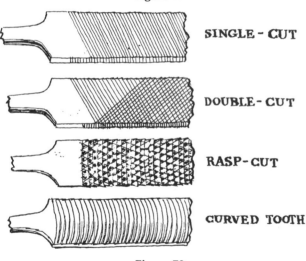

SINGLE-CUT

DOUBLE-CUT

RASP-CUT

CURVED TOOTH

Figure 78.

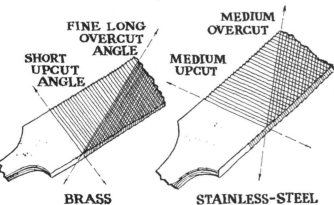

FINE LONG
OVERCUT
ANGLE

MEDIUM
OVERCUT

SHORT
UPCUT
ANGLE

MEDIUM
UPCUT

BRASS

STAINLESS-STEEL

Figure 79.

man double-bevel, and the tradesman single-bevel hatchets. Most of these are used for specific tasks. A shaping tool for general purpose use in the homestead workshop is the double-beveled half hatchet, which has a heavy butt opposing its blade (Fig. 76).

For more accurate wood shaping, a homesteader should consider the merit of using a drawknife (Fig. 77). Prior to smoothing wood with a plane, a drawknife is often used to shape it from its rough-hewn state. (Having exhausted the subject of wood planing in Chapter 1, we will go on to a discussion of filing wood and metals.)

A file is a hand tool of hardened steel, with sharp cutting edges across its face, usually diagonal to its axis (see Figure 78). This tool is made in a variety of sizes, shapes, and grades of cut. With over 3000 variations from which to choose, it may seem impossible to select only those files appropriate for the adequately equipped homestead workshop. Therefore, some classification is necessary; the most basic divides file work into shaping wood or shaping metals. Next, there are two kinds of cutting surfaces or teeth: chisel-toothed or rasp-cut. Either of these file surfaces can be used to shape wood but only the chisel-toothed file may be used to file metal. The rasp-cut surface abrades (rubs or wears away) material whereas a chisel-toothed surface cuts (gouges or carves) material. The longer the file, the coarser its teeth. For example, rough shaping is first done with a 16-inch rasp and then refined with a 6-inch rasp.

Soft metals, such as lead, brass, and aluminum, will clog a fine-toothed file, so files with special configuration must be used to shape these metals. Lead-soldered joints, for example, may be smoothed with a single-cut float file; its teeth are coarse like a rasp and the angle of their cut is slight so that it virtually shaves away lead filings. The depth of cut and the angle of file teeth are designed specifically to shape particular metals (Fig. 79). A fine, long angle of overcut prevents chips from accumulating between file teeth. A file used to rough-shape aluminum has a deep upcut and a fine overcut. To prevent a worker from grooving a soft material like brass, the angle of overcut is long and fine but the angle of upcut is short. For stainless steel, the angles of overcut and undercut are about the same.

Files are further classified as having either single-cut or double-cut teeth. With a single-cut file, teeth are set in parallel rows at an angle of about 65 degrees to the axis of the file (see Figure 80). The deeper and wider these spacings, the coarser is the file. Single-cut files deliver a finish smoother than that given by double-cut files. When soft metals or wood must be smoothed, a single-cut file with a long angle of incision delivers a shearing cut. Most salespeople of hardware products know this tool as a "shear-toothed" file.

More precise, descriptive nomenclature for files is based on the number of teeth per inch. A "coarse" file has from twenty to twenty-five teeth, depending on the length of the file. A "middle" file has from twenty-five to thirty teeth per inch. A "bastard" file has from thirty to forty teeth per inch; a second-cut file, from forty to fifty; a smooth file, from fifty to sixty; and a dead smooth file has a hundred or more teeth per inch. This classification applies to both single-cut and double-cut files. It also applies to the six different shapes of file (Fig. 81), whether round, half-round, triangular or three-square, crosscut or square, flat, and tapered or warding, like the mill file. The longer the file, the rougher the cut. The amount of space in which it may be used also affects one's selection.

For general homestead shopwork, one needs only three common files, namely, the *bastard,* the *second-cut,* and the *smooth* file (Fig. 82). Round holes are best shaped with round files. Curved material may be formed using a half-round file. A triangular file is useful for restoring damaged, irregular saw teeth or threads. Body and fender work calls for a file with curved teeth, which is also excellent for most sheet-metal work. The thin warding file has uniform thickness and tapers to fit narrow spaces.

The mainstay of virtually all precision metal-filing tasks in shopwork is the mill file, so called because it was first used to sharpen circular saw blades in lumber mills. Tapered in thickness and width, it has only a single-cut pattern and

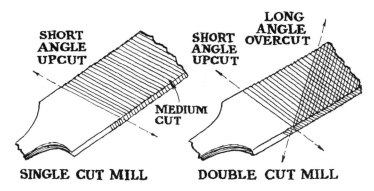

Figure 80.

FILE TYPES

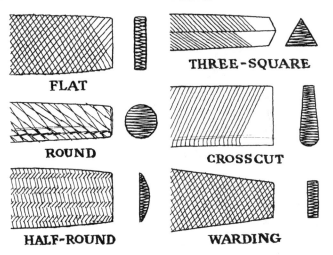

Figure 81.

COMPARATIVE COARSENESS OF 10-INCH FILES

SINGLE CUT MILL

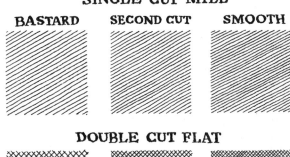

DOUBLE CUT FLAT

Figure 82.

CORRECT POSITION OF BODY IN FILING

Figure 83.

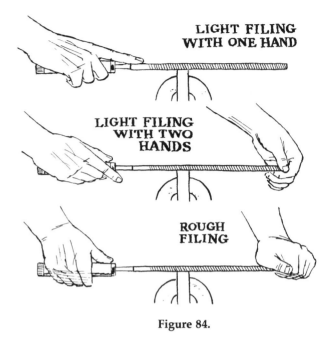

LIGHT FILING WITH ONE HAND

LIGHT FILING WITH TWO HANDS

ROUGH FILING

Figure 84.

one edge has no teeth. This "safe edge" lends itself to the sharpening of saw blades and similar kinds of tool blades.

A more general all-purpose abrasive tool is either the flat or the hand file, each differing only in thickness and taper. Flat files are made with either a single-cut or a double-cut pattern.

When filing, as with any other shop activity, it is as important to use the tool properly as it is to make its selection. Work must be securely anchored at the proper working height. For the right-handed person, the feet should be spread well apart, with the left foot in advance of the right (Fig. 83). The way the file is held depends on the amount of material to be removed. The more firmly the file is gripped, the more weight the worker will be able to place on the tool (see Figure 84). If an even surface is desired, your weight should be evenly distributed as the file passes over the length of the work. For accuracy, guidance with your hands is essential in order to keep the file level and steady in its movement. As a file moves over the work, your weight shifts as you transfer equal amounts of

pressure from one hand to the other, so that equal pressure is exerted for the length of the stroke. Pressure is applied only on the forward stroke. When it is pushed across the work, the file should be moved diagonally over the surface to insure a flat, evenly finished appearance (Fig. 85). When using single-cut files for the smooth finishing of soft metals, there is a tendency for this file to slide to the left because of the long upcut angle of its teeth. This trend can be offset by guiding the stroke diagonally somewhat to the right.

Since file teeth do not cut on the back stroke, they tend to become clogged with loose filings. Thus, on this stroke the file should be lifted lightly from the surface of the work.

Files without handles should never be used. We prefer an adjustable handle that securely grips a file, like that illustrated in Figure 86. A file brush or card (Fig. 87) must also be readily available so that files may be cleaned before they are "racked" (Fig. 88). Racking is the preferred way to protect files, for when they are loosely piled in a drawer, they tend to become dulled or even damaged. True, files are hard-surfaced but individual teeth are nonetheless fine and brittle.

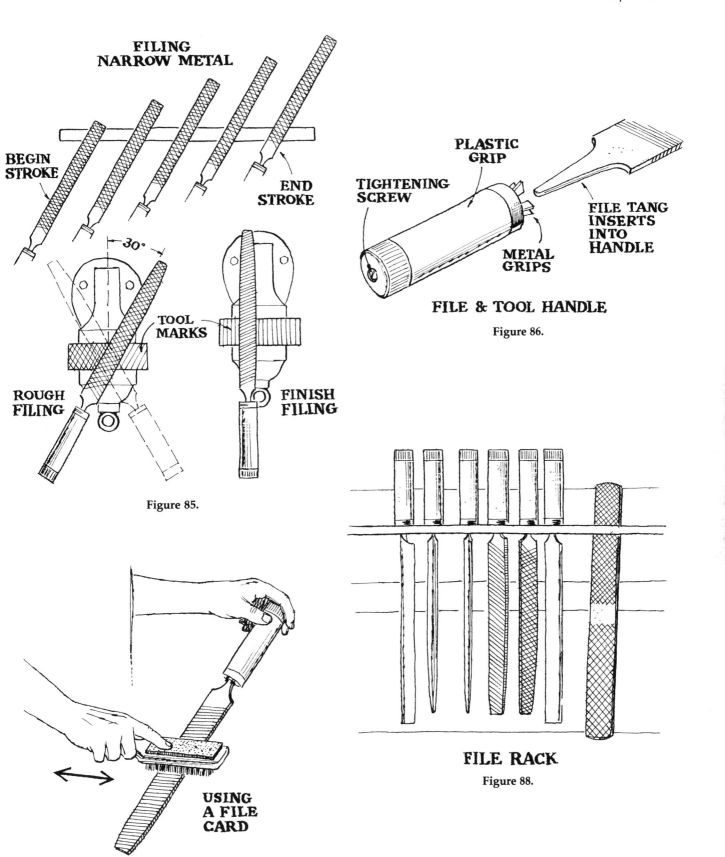

FILING NARROW METAL

BEGIN STROKE

END STROKE

30°

TOOL MARKS

ROUGH FILING

FINISH FILING

Figure 85.

PLASTIC GRIP

TIGHTENING SCREW

METAL GRIPS

FILE TANG INSERTS INTO HANDLE

FILE & TOOL HANDLE

Figure 86.

USING A FILE CARD

Figure 87.

FILE RACK

Figure 88.

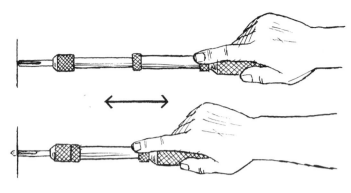

PUSH DRILL

Figure 89.

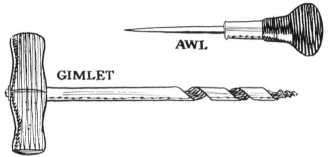

AWL

GIMLET

Figure 90.

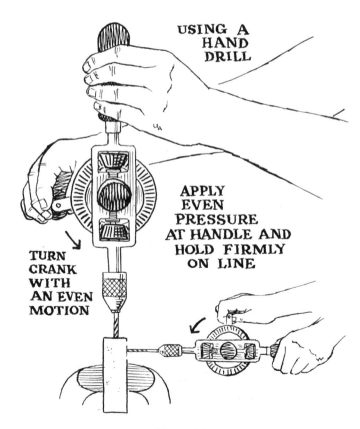

USING A HAND DRILL

APPLY EVEN PRESSURE AT HANDLE AND HOLD FIRMLY ON LINE

TURN CRANK WITH AN EVEN MOTION

Figure 91.

Chapter 6
DRILLING TOOLS

The portable electric drill is in such widespread use today that we forget workers drilled holes in wood and metal centuries before Edison harnessed electricity to run power drills. There is, in fact, a handheld push drill (also known as an Archimedean drill after its ancient Greek inventor), which rotates as one slides the handle up and down a spiral stem with one hand (Fig. 89). The other hand remains free to hold the work. Simpler yet is the scratch awl (Fig. 90), a pointed tool used to make small starting holes in wood which is to receive either screws or nails. When a winding cutting edge was added to the shaft of the awl, a new drill tool was created. Called the gimlet, this tool is a super awl, which is also used to start screws and nails. Similar in design to the drill, the gimlet has a twisting point that shapes or threads screw holes.

To accurately drill metal as well as wood, the homesteader should use a hand drill (Fig. 91). With this tool, you can actually *feel* several distinct levels of the drilling operation. For example, as the right hand turns the crank in a steady motion, gradually increasing the speed of rotation, the left hand applies even pressure. Control of the cutting process using your sense of feel is possible with a hand drill, for you sense the drill bit as it begins to protrude through the material. Thus pressure and speed are reduced, preventing the drill bit from being shoved precipitately through the newly cut hole, resulting in the drill bit's being dulled or broken.

To drill large holes in metal, you should use a breast drill (Fig. 92), so called because of its adjustable plate against which greater body pressure may be applied. One of the two handles of this drill is longer to provide more turning torque, or motion. The drill is equipped with two-speed drive.

When greater turning motion is necessary to drill wider, longer holes in wood, a carpenter's brace (Fig. 93) may be used to advantage. Turning force results from twisting the frame of the tool, a drilling concept first used in the fourteenth century by European carpenters. At that time, each brace was permanently equipped with a different-sized bit. Two hundred years passed before someone devised a chuck, or clamp, that would enable different-sized bits to be used in a single brace. Another two hundred years passed before someone else developed a ratchet, or hinged catch, that permitted use of the brace in constricted places.

Whether drilling through hard metal or soft wood, the properly sharpened bit of the hand-powered tool can be both responsive and reliable. Power drills are useful for production work, but for most homestead tasks hand drills are entirely satisfactory. Holes in hard metal over an inch in diameter may even be drilled by hand if one has a post drill (Fig. 94). This tool, forerunner of the common electric drill press, reached a high degree of technological sophistication before its replacement earlier this

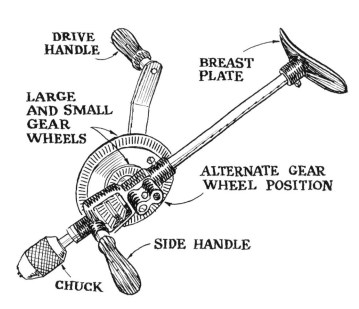

BREAST DRILL

Figure 92.

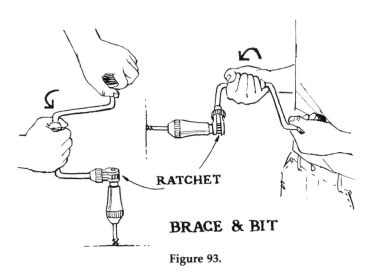

BRACE & BIT

Figure 93.

century. Even though it was hand-cranked, the post drill had an automatic self-feed and three gears with double-journal ball bearings, which provided higher speeds while its turning direction remained the same as for lower speeds. As the drill continued in motion, a quick-return lever (previously set) raised the bit from the work and stopped drilling action automatically.

A modern workshop will more likely have a drill stand that holds a portable electric drill, transforming it into a drill press. Removed from this frame, the drill may be converted into a number of useful tools: a saber saw, water pump, drill-bit sharpener, drum sander, paint mixer, rotary file and rasp, wire brush, or grinder.

The type and sharpness of the drill bit, however, is more important to the drilling process than whether or not an electric motor is used to power the tool. The most common bit used for drilling metal is the twist drill. Close inspection of this drill bit (Fig. 95) shows why many professional machinists think it is the most efficient tool in the shop. In no other bit is the cutting surface so great in proportion to its cross-sectional area; when forming the twisting flutes, about half the original metal shank is removed although this area bears more stress in proportion to its strength. These flutes have three functions: to form the cutting edge on the cone-shaped point, to allow chips to move up out of the hole, and to permit lubricant to reach the cutting edge. Flutes are separated from one another by a metal shaft, called the web. Its thickness varies throughout the length of the drill bit, being heavier near the shank or neck—that part between the handle and the working part—where more support and strength are needed. At the outer edge of the drill bit a narrow strip, called the margin, runs full length along the flute. The body of the drill bit is actually of lesser diameter than this margin. Thus, more lubricant reaches the drill point through the space called body clearance. There is also less friction against the narrow margin than there would be if the entire shank made contact with the drill hole.

The vital part of a twist drill, its cutting edge,

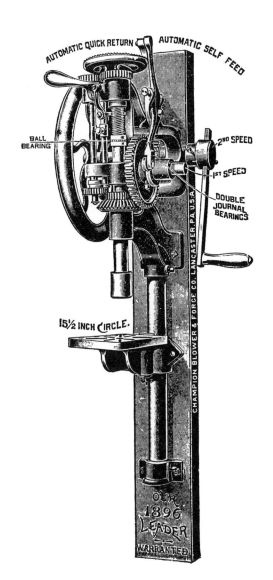

**CHAMPION QUICK ~ RETURN
SELF ~ FEED POST DRILL**

Figure 94.

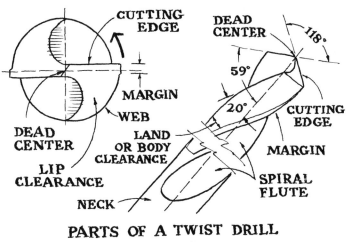

PARTS OF A TWIST DRILL

Figure 95.

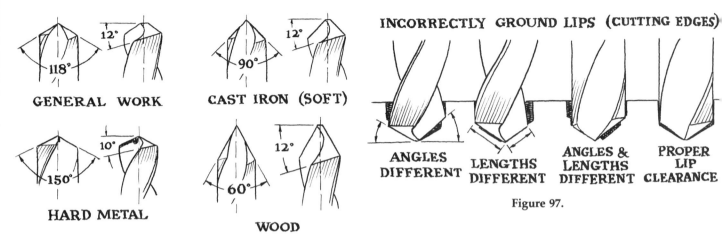

Figure 96.

Figure 97.

must be properly sharpened. If insufficient clearance is allowed, the cutting lip will be in constant contact with metal during drilling, preventing the lip from biting into the metal or making it rub against, but not penetrate, the metal.

For proper cutting action, the surface behind the lips of the drill bit must be ground away to give the bit "relief." Years of trial and error have determined the optimum angle of this relief to be 12 degrees (Fig. 96). If the angle for lip clearance is ground to more than 12 degrees, edges of the cutting lip will likely break off due to insufficient support. When ground to less than 12 degrees, penetration is hampered and the bit may split up its center. The angle for the point should be 59 degrees.

Of equal importance is the need to have both lips ground the same length. If this is not done, the drill bit will bind on one side at the point where the cutting angles differ (Fig. 97). Binding may result from using a burned drill bit, for one side will be doing all the cutting and will soon overheat. When cutting angles are equal but of different lengths, the drill hole will become much larger than the bit, wearing away the bit and straining the drill.

The final consideration for proper use of a twist drill involves the speed and pressure that must be exerted to operate it. Again, pressure or feed into the material can best be felt. If the metal is hard, the rate of feed should be slowed and speed reduced. A drill bit of large diameter should revolve more slowly than a small one. If it revolves too rapidly, its metal is apt to overheat and lose temper or strength.

Auger bits, those used in a carpenter's brace to drill wood, are not as elaborate in design or in need of as critical sharpening as are the bits of a metalworking twist drill. Three general types of auger bits are available as illustrated in Figure 98. The most common one is the double spur, which is used when a smooth, clean hole is desired and rapid cutting speed is unnecessary. A single-spur auger bit is known for its cutting speed; with a solid center, it is stiffer and more useful for drilling deep holes. The third type of auger bit has a hollow center that removes considerable amounts of material. It is used to rapidly drill deep holes. Each of these bits has a screw point which literally pulls the bit into wood. The depth of cut from each revolution of the bit corresponds to the pitch of the screw thread (Fig. 99). A steep pitch of the drill point cuts fast, makes large chips, but is harder to turn. A shallow pitch cuts thin chips, is easy to turn in a brace, but is slow to operate.

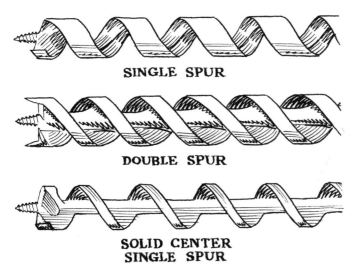

SINGLE SPUR

DOUBLE SPUR

SOLID CENTER
SINGLE SPUR

Figure 98.

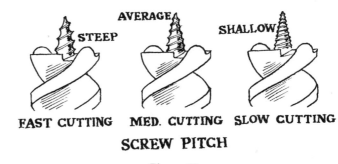

STEEP   AVERAGE   SHALLOW

FAST CUTTING   MED. CUTTING   SLOW CUTTING

SCREW PITCH

Figure 99.

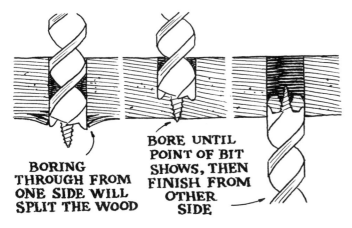

BORING
THROUGH FROM
ONE SIDE WILL
SPLIT THE WOOD

BORE UNTIL
POINT OF BIT
SHOWS, THEN
FINISH FROM
OTHER
SIDE

Figure 100.

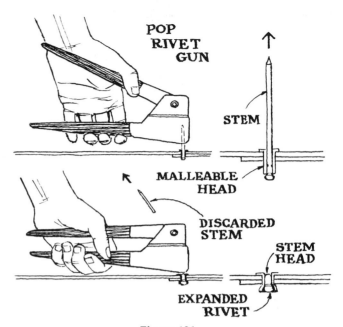

POP RIVET GUN

STEM

MALLEABLE HEAD

DISCARDED STEM

STEM HEAD

EXPANDED RIVET

Figure 101.

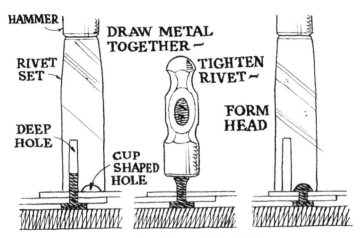

HAMMER

DRAW METAL TOGETHER ~

RIVET SET

TIGHTEN RIVET ~

FORM HEAD

DEEP HOLE

CUP SHAPED HOLE

USING A RIVET SET

Figure 102.

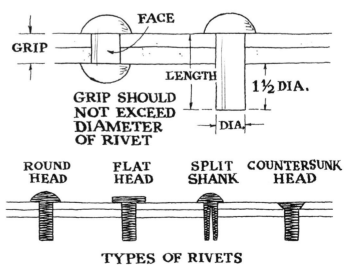

FACE

GRIP

LENGTH

1½ DIA.

DIA.

GRIP SHOULD NOT EXCEED DIAMETER OF RIVET

ROUND HEAD   FLAT HEAD   SPLIT SHANK   COUNTERSUNK HEAD

TYPES OF RIVETS

Figure 103.

Chapter 7
FASTENING TOOLS AND TECHNIQUES

One obvious thing about homestead shopwork is that there are many different ways to fasten materials together. To join pieces of metal, some people weld while others prefer to bolt. Still others enjoy using the pop riveter. When joining pieces of wood, some people prefer to screw or bolt members rather than nail or glue them. Actually, these and many other fastening methods have both advantages and disadvantages.

It is important to know the full range of fastening techniques and to have the tools and the know-how to perform each one. Knowledge of the cost of the fastener unit and the effort needed to apply it should also precede the start of the work. A pop riveter, for instance, is a particularly important device if one side of the articles being joined is inaccessible, for they can then be "blind" riveted. The handheld rivet gun pulls on the stem of a rivet, which spreads a malleable head on the unreachable underside of the material (Fig. 101). On its way out of the gun, the stem of the rivet breaks off. As might be imagined, the cost of the individual rivet fastener is high. To do ordinary flat work, it is less costly to use a rivet set (Fig. 102) driven by a ball peen hammer. Prior to riveting, one must first decide whether to use solid, hollow, or split-shank rivets, also choosing between those with a round, flat, or countersunk head (Fig. 103).

It is a simple matter to select the size of rivet to use. Its diameter should not be less than the combined thickness of the sheets being joined, and its length should extend one and one-half diameters beyond the face of the material. Rivets are made of many kinds of metal, for it is often necessary to use a rivet made of the same material as that being fastened.

A rivet set may be used to draw pieces of sheet metal together, and a ball peen hammer is used to form the head of the rivet, as illustrated in Figure 102. Hammers used to fasten materials together vary in weight and type (Fig. 105); the ball peen is used for metal work and the claw hammer for woodworking. The former is specially hardened for its purpose. Frequently, a soft-face hammer is needed in the homestead shop to drive a wood chisel or to form soft metal. Of the two nailing hammers available, the straight claw is best for out-of-shop construction carpentry, while the curved claw is best for general shopwork.

It is common for those beginning mechanical repair work to misuse even the most basic of hand tools, the hammer. They usually hold the hammer handle too close to its head (Fig. 106), "choking" or blocking the hammer's full swing and reducing the force of its blow. This throttling of the hammer also prevents its impacting parallel to the work since its head is at an angle to the object being hammered. This prevents an even distribution of the force of the blow over the full face of the hammer, often causing damage to the hammer face and the surface of the

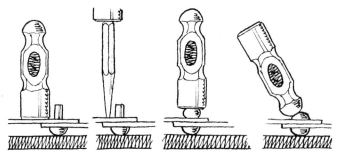

USING LARGE RIVETS

Figure 104.

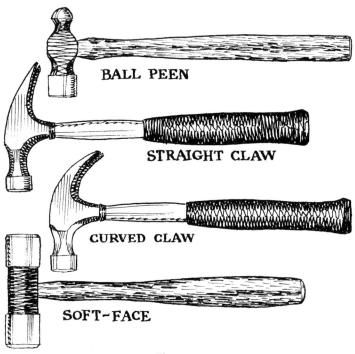

BALL PEEN

STRAIGHT CLAW

CURVED CLAW

SOFT-FACE

Figure 105.

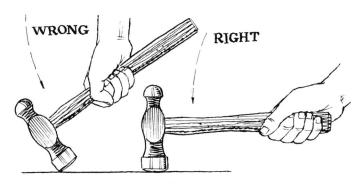

WRONG   RIGHT

Figure 106.

work. Rest your thumb on the hammer handle so that it does not overlap the fingers, which should grip the handle alongside the thumb.

Perhaps the most basic of all tools used to fasten pliable materials is the staple gun, especially adaptable since one hand is freed to hold material while the other operates the gun (Fig. 107). Driving power for the stapler comes from a large spring, which is cocked and released when you squeeze the handle downward. Staples give excellent holding power and can be rapidly driven into thin, malleable materials.

When thick wooden pieces must be fastened securely, you may choose from a wide variety of nails, or when either wood or metal needs to be attached, you may choose from a variety of screws. An outcome of World War II aircraft construction was the development of the hardened self-tapping sheet-metal screw, an article especially useful for joining pieces of light-gauge sheet metal. No drilling is necessary, for the metal is simply clean-punched with a stop punch, chosen from various sizes. The point of the punch selected will be gauged to fit the thickness of the metal and the diameter of the screw (Fig. 108).

Customarily, a screwdriver is used to drive or remove screws, yet this tool varies enormously in its available designs and sizes. We tend to be skeptical of new tools of unorthodox design, so when the EasyDriver screwdriver (Fig. 110) appeared on the market, our suspicion was that this, too, would be just another gimmick tool. However, after using it repeatedly, we have discovered that this tool has important design features especially applicable for homestead-shop use. We found, for instance, that its ball-shaped handle gives twice the turning power of that given by the standard screwdriver. Designed to fit the palm of the hand, the spherical handle of this contemporary tool has more area of contact with the hand. Because a ratchet is built into the handle, one side of it may be used to drive screws and the other to remove them. Furthermore, various inexpensive bits snap into the shaft, eliminating the need to buy multiple screwdrivers to equip your homestead shop.

It is important to match the tip of the driver to the size of the screw slot; if the slot is larger

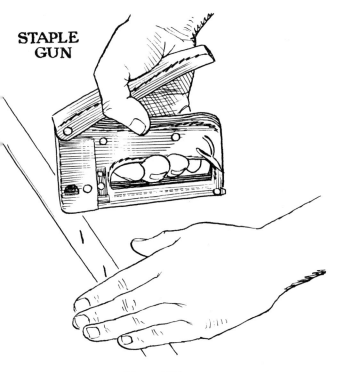

STAPLE GUN

Figure 107.

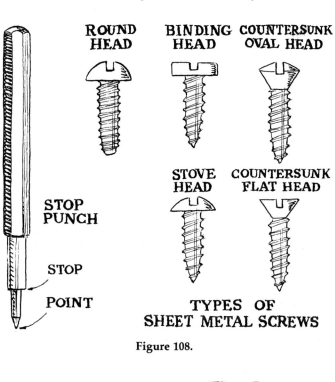

ROUND HEAD
BINDING HEAD
COUNTERSUNK OVAL HEAD

STOVE HEAD
COUNTERSUNK FLAT HEAD

STOP PUNCH

STOP

POINT

TYPES OF SHEET METAL SCREWS

Figure 108.

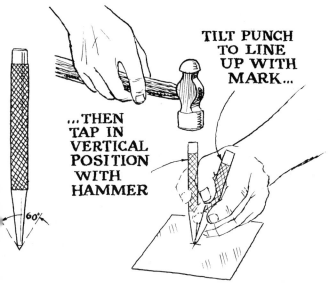

TILT PUNCH TO LINE UP WITH MARK...

...THEN TAP IN VERTICAL POSITION WITH HAMMER

60%

USING A CENTER PUNCH

Figure 109.

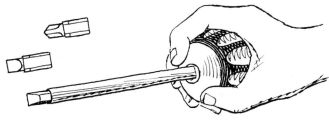

"EASYDRIVER"

Figure 110.

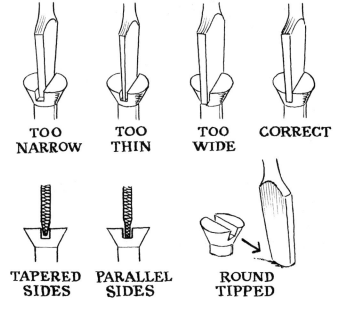

TOO NARROW
TOO THIN
TOO WIDE
CORRECT

TAPERED SIDES
PARALLEL SIDES
ROUND TIPPED

Figure 111.

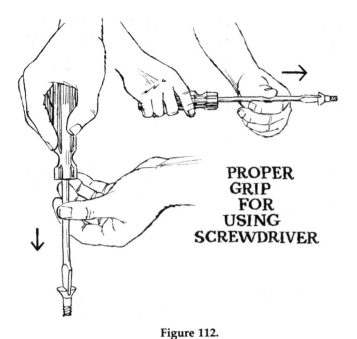

PROPER GRIP FOR USING SCREWDRIVER

Figure 112.

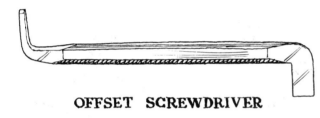

OFFSET SCREWDRIVER

Figure 113.

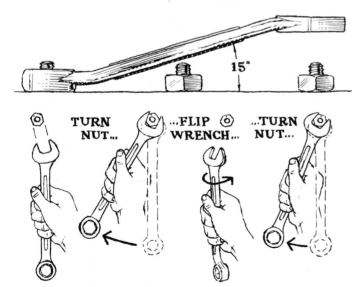

15°

TURN NUT...   ...FLIP WRENCH...   ...TURN NUT...

USING BOX WRENCH IN RESTRICTED SPACE

Figure 114.

than the blade of the screwdriver, it may become burred when the driver slips in the slot as it is turned (Fig. 111). If sides of the blade taper too much, the driver may lift off the screw when twist is applied. Several decades ago, industry fashioned and mass produced a screw called a Phillips head, which was designed to be driven with power equipment, decreasing the possibility for blade lift-off, for slippage, and damage to work. This self-centering screw is particularly suitable for production-line work. But in homestead shopwork this screw head is inconvenient, for its use requires that the shopworker stock yet another type of screwdriver in various sizes.

An offset screwdriver is handy for use in constricted, hard-to-reach places. Called "offset" because its two ends are offset at right angles to the shank and at right angles to each other, it enables you to turn a screw that is more or less inaccessible (Fig. 113).

Some wrenches are offset as well, enabling them to be used in constricted places. The wrench is merely turned over each time the nut is moved, as illustrated in Figure 114. The combination wrench has an open end and a "box" end, which engages all six corners of a nut. The latter is less likely to slip and is often used to loosen or tighten a nut. Reversed, the open end may be used to turn a nut more quickly. The offset of the box end of this wrench provides clearance above nearby objects.

The adjustable or Crescent wrench (Fig. 115) is every homesteader's standby tool. It has both a stationary and an adjustable jaw, enabling it to fit various sizes of nut. This wrench should always be turned in the direction of its movable jaw. Otherwise, instead of tightening the wrench on the nut as it is turned, it will loosen and slip. When it is turned toward the movable jaw, forces of torque are absorbed in the body of its fixed jaw, not its weaker tip.

A socket wrench is but a refinement of the box wrench. Its socket has a square opening or tubular recess into which a square drive lug on a detachable handle is fitted. The most useful of detachable assemblies for this tool is probably the ratchet handle (Fig. 116), with which it is

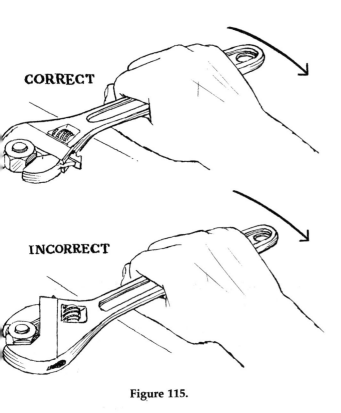

CORRECT

INCORRECT

Figure 115.

possible to tighten or loosen a nut without removing the handle. When more leverage is necessary, a breaker bar may be fitted to a socket wrench. Other useful accessories include bar extensions, adapters, a speed handle, and universal joints. Bar extensions lengthen the distance between the socket and the handle. A speed handle, used like a woodworker's brace, removes or replaces nuts rapidly. Adapters fit a handle, with a drive on one size, to a socket that has a different-size drive. For example, a ½-inch by ⅜-inch adapter makes it possible to turn any ⅜-inch socket with any ½-inch handle. A universal-joint socket turns a nut while the wrench handle is held at an angle.

To fasten round pipe or pipe fittings, an adjustable pipe wrench, called a Stillson wrench, is customarily used. Its movable jaw pivots to grip a pipe or a fitting. Place the pipe at the back part of the jaws and regulate the adjustment screw so that it gives the jaws a firm grip on the pipe. As pressure is applied to the handle with the right hand, the adjustable jaw should be pressed firmly with the left hand, as illustrated in Figure 117. This action helps the teeth of the wrench bite into the pipe. Serrations on each jaw are angled in opposing directions.

Fastening tools should include those used to solder, braze, and weld metals. No homestead shop would be complete without ways in which to unite two pieces of metal with an alloyed metal. Due to the complexity of this operation, it will be discussed in Part III.

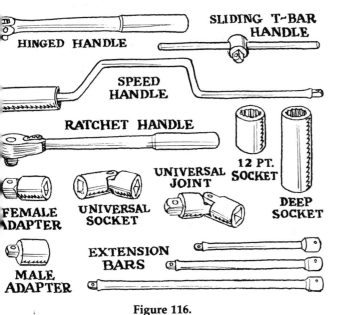

HINGED HANDLE

SLIDING T-BAR HANDLE

SPEED HANDLE

RATCHET HANDLE

12 PT. SOCKET

UNIVERSAL JOINT

UNIVERSAL SOCKET

DEEP SOCKET

FEMALE ADAPTER

MALE ADAPTER

EXTENSION BARS

Figure 116.

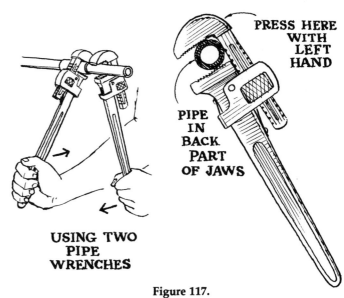

PRESS HERE WITH LEFT HAND

PIPE IN BACK PART OF JAWS

USING TWO PIPE WRENCHES

Figure 117.

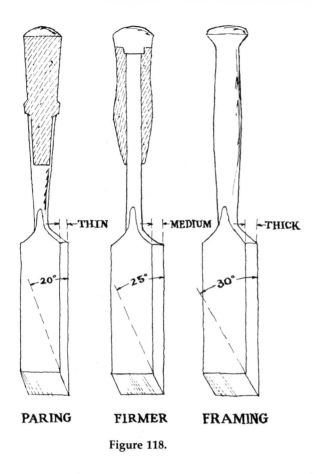

PARING   FIRMER   FRAMING

Figure 118.

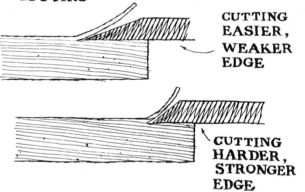

HOW SHARPENING ANGLE AFFECTS CUTTING

CUTTING EASIER, WEAKER EDGE

CUTTING HARDER, STRONGER EDGE

Figure 119.

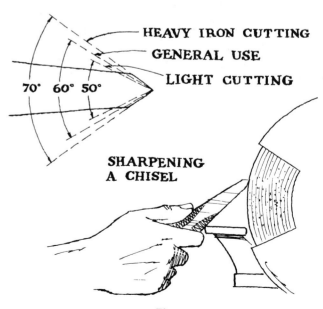

HEAVY IRON CUTTING

GENERAL USE

LIGHT CUTTING

70° 60° 50°

SHARPENING A CHISEL

Figure 120.

Chapter 8
SHARPENING TOOLS

Included under the subject heading of tool sharpening are other methods for the preventive maintenance of hand tools. It is important for the homesteader to consistently care for and repair all tools that play their part in sustaining homestead life. Broken or dulled tools tend to be handled improperly in order to compensate for their damage or lack of a keen edge. Also, energy is unnecessarily expended to achieve expected results, with this added effort often culminating in error or accident. Tools in disrepair may cause frustration, risk safety, and compromise performance. On the other hand, expectations of satisfaction run high when raw material begins to respond to a well-cared-for tool.

Before you can maintain or repair any tool, you must understand how that tool works when put to its optimum use. If this knowledge is lacking, you undoubtedly will not know how to keep the tool functioning properly. In our shop, for example, we have three types of wood chisel—those used for light, medium, or heavy work (Fig. 118). The lightweight *paring chisel* has an all-wood handle, is pushed by hand, and its cutting edge is sharpened with an oblique bevel of 20 degrees. The medium-weighted utility chisel, the *firmer*, has a wooden handle with a metal core capped by an iron ferrule. This hewing tool is worked with a wooden mallet and its cutting edge of 25 degrees is blunt. The heavy-duty *framing chisel* is made entirely of metal, has a bevel of 30 degrees, and is struck with an ordinary metal hammer in order to

gouge or remove large quantities of material. Significantly, the hardness of material to be chiseled and the angle of the cutting edge determine which chisel should be used for any one particular job (see Figure 119). For instance, we previously noted that a block plane cuts hardwood best when the angle of its blade is 12 degrees above the horizon line. When working softwood, this angle should be greater, or 20 degrees, for either type of tool.

The hardness of material to be shaped and the cutting edge chosen to chisel it are the chief factors involved in metal cutting. The well-equipped homestead shop needs two kinds of cold (or metal-cutting) chisels, one to shape heavy iron stock and one for thin sheet metal. The cutting edge of metal chisels should vary from 50 degrees for work on light material to 70 degrees for work on heavier metals (Fig. 120). The tapered end of any of the center punches, which are used to start or align holes drilled in either hard or soft metals, is beveled to an intermediate angle of 60 degrees.

An angle of 59 degrees has long been established as that appropriate to the twist drill (Fig. 121), which is used to bore mild steel. (This angle is the result of centuries of experimentation, and occasionally the homesteader would do well to contemplate tool history and the evolution of tool design, the importance of which we too often take for granted.) To drill wood, a setting of 70 degrees may be required, whereas to drill tempered steel, a 30-degree angle may

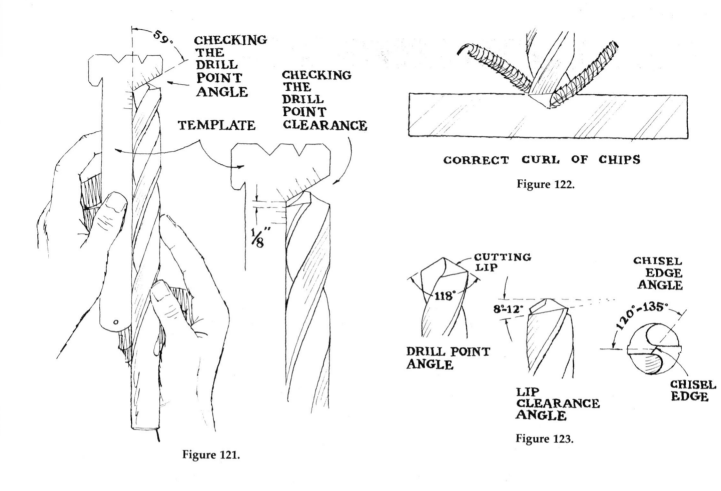

Figure 121.

CORRECT CURL OF CHIPS

Figure 122.

Figure 123.

be sufficient. But a drill bit angle of 59 degrees remains the universal standard for boring holes in the wider range of metals. At this setting, two continuous strands of shavings are extruded as a twist drill penetrates material (Fig. 122).

A twist drill has two cutting lips, and some clearance under each lip is necessary so that the forward cutting surface may remove chips of the material. This angle of clearance, called the lip-relief angle, is about 10 degrees (Fig. 123). If the lip-clearance angle is, for example, less than 5 degrees, the cutting edge will not bore and will not produce a chip. If lip clearance is more than an angle of 12 degrees, the cutting edge is significantly weakened by the removal of too much metal behind it.

As wood or metal is bored, flutes that spiral about the body of the twist drill and furnish the cutting edges remove chips from the drill hole. It is important to grind equally both sides of the cutting angle as well as both sides of the lip-relief angle. If they are not identical, the drill point will be thrown off center, causing it to wobble and bore a hole larger than required. If cutting edges are not ground the same, one lip does all the work, overheats, and dulls rapidly when used.

A template or gauge of some kind must be used by the shopworker to determine the proper bevel for drill bits. We use a 59-degree drill-point gauge that includes a built-in bevel protractor. With this tool we can, at the same time, check both the cutting angle and the length of the cutting edge. It is a useful device with which to regulate the proper angles for cutting edges for woodworking as well as metalworking tools (Fig. 124).

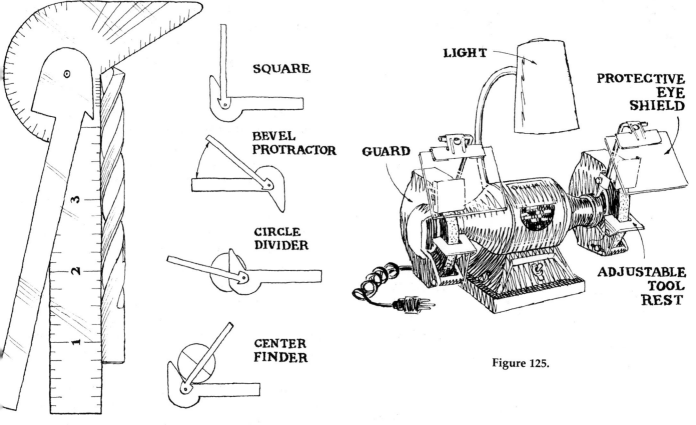

MULTI-USE RULE & GAGE

SQUARE

BEVEL PROTRACTOR

CIRCLE DIVIDER

CENTER FINDER

LIGHT

GUARD

PROTECTIVE EYE SHIELD

ADJUSTABLE TOOL REST

Figure 124.

Figure 125.

The bench grinder (Fig. 125) has a flat circular stone mounted on a spindle that is turned by a winch handle or a treadle or is powered by electricity. This is the best all-around choice for a tool to shape and sharpen metalworking tools. The grinding process is one that wears down the cutting surface of hand tools by the abrasive action of thousands of grains of either aluminum oxide or silicon carbide bonded by an agent such as rubber. Tool sharpening is done primarily on a grinding wheel consisting of grains of aluminum oxide.

The bonding agent used in a grindstone is as important as its abrasive element, for strength of the stone depends on this connective or binding element. Thin cutoff wheels used to cut metal require a grindstone bonded with rubber to provide strength without brittleness. For large wheels turning at slow speed, a grindstone with silicate bond is desirable. Low-speed turning prevents metal from heating as it is ground and prevents its losing temper or hardness. Furthermore, a silicate bonding agent is relatively soft so that abrasive grains are more readily cast off as tool blades or tool points sharpen, preventing the clogging of grindstone pores.

Almost all high-speed grinding wheels use a grindstone with a vitrified or heat-fused bond. Strong yet porous, temperature changes have little effect on this stone. Nor does the introduction of oil or water to its surface during the grinding process affect it. There are about thirty grades of abrasive surface—from coarse-grained to very fine-grained—which may be purchased when one goes to buy a grinding wheel for the homestead shop. In general, the harder the metal, the finer grained the grind-

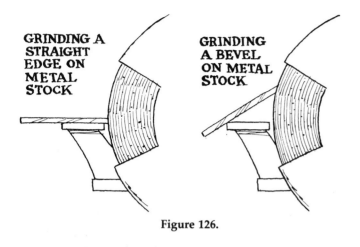

GRINDING A STRAIGHT EDGE ON METAL STOCK

GRINDING A BEVEL ON METAL STOCK

Figure 126.

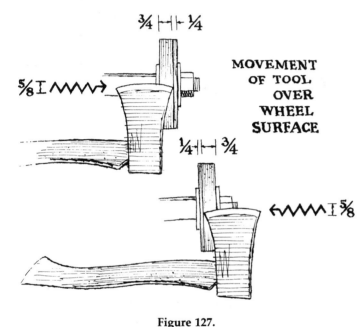

MOVEMENT OF TOOL OVER WHEEL SURFACE

Figure 127.

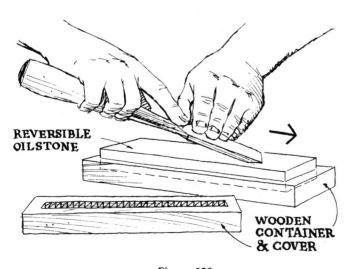

REVERSIBLE OILSTONE

WOODEN CONTAINER & COVER

Figure 128.

stone should be. Coarse-grained stones are handy for removing sizable amounts of soft metal, but they would be unsatisfactory for sharpening metal blades; the metal surface thus cut would be too rough to properly finish. A medium-fine grain, of about size 60, is recommended for tool sharpening. Abrasives in this stone should coalesce with a soft grade of bonding agent; that is, the stone should contain a small amount of bond relative to the amount of abrasive used. Then, as a blade is sharpened, there is little resistance to the pressure exerted, for abrasive grains are not firmly bound and less heat buildup occurs in the metal being sharpened.

In addition, as a metal tool is ground it should be frequently dipped in water to prevent its overheating. The metal should also pass slowly across the face of the grinding wheel so that the entire width of the blade is ground in a single movement in any one direction. This, too, prevents the metal from being overheated and prevents the grindstone from wearing unevenly.

When the cutting edge of a tool is nicked or a new bevel is necessary, grinding is mandatory. Useful for preliminary shaping and removing major surface imperfections, grinding wheels nevertheless have their limitations. The final keen edge on any cutting tool must be honed on an oilstone (Fig. 128), a repetitive ongoing process especially with woodworking tools. Only rarely is it necessary to grind a woodworking tool on a grinding wheel.

We prefer to use a manufactured carborundum oilstone, one with a fine grit on one side of the stone and a coarse grit on the other. The tool is first rapidly sharpened on the coarse side of the stone and then smoothed to a keen edge on the other side, as illustrated with the chisel in Figure 129. Oil is the coolant applied to the surface of the oilstone to prevent friction from heat buildup in the metal being ground. The oil also, in effect, floats off metal and stone particles that result.

A mixture of kerosene and light motor oil may be used to lubricate an oilstone, for pores of the stone are then less apt to fill with metal particles. As the cutting edge is drawn back and forth over the surface of the oil-saturated stone, movement should be parallel with the long edge of the stone. This requires that your hands be steady. Use the full face of the stone when sharpening, so that the center of the oilstone is not prematurely hollowed out. The stone should be wiped dry when sharpening is finished and should be kept covered to protect it from dirt and grime.

Early pioneer homesteaders were familiar with the old adage "There's no time lost in whetting." Those were the days when sharpened axes were needed to efficiently clear land and when sharpened scythes were essential to harvest grain crops. Even today, a keen-edged axe continues to be the most important tool on the homestead, perhaps above all others the symbol of homestead living. A recent tool catalog illustrates a dozen different types of both hatchets and axes. Each blade has its own unique characteristics, depending upon the use to which it is put (Fig. 130). For example, a thin blade with a long bevel is ideal for chopping. A blade sharpened only on one side may best be used for hewing or shaping. One with a thick blade and short bevel is valuable for splitting. When sharpening a hatchet or axe, be sure to retain the original curvature of the blade. A grinding wheel may be used for crude reshaping, but many mechanics feel that the final beveled surface should be made with a smooth mill file. Use of a grindstone is thought to overheat the edge of the blade, causing it to lose temper or hardness.

Besides hatchets and axes, many tools in the workshop are sharpened with some form of steel file. An auger-bit file is manufactured solely to sharpen wood-boring auger bits. One side of the file, the safe-faced side, is serrated on its edges, and the other, the safe-edged side, has serrations on its surface (Fig. 131).

A three-cornered file, called the triangular taper file, will put an edge on the teeth of hand saws. The round rat-tail file is used to file the blade of a chain saw, and a single-cut file, shaped like a wedge with one round edge, will sharpen circular saw blades.

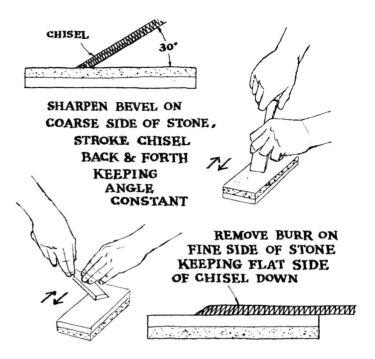

SHARPEN BEVEL ON COARSE SIDE OF STONE. STROKE CHISEL BACK & FORTH KEEPING ANGLE CONSTANT

REMOVE BURR ON FINE SIDE OF STONE KEEPING FLAT SIDE OF CHISEL DOWN

SHARPENING A WOODWORKER'S CHISEL

Figure 129.

SOFTWOOD 25°

HARDWOOD 45°

HEWING A LINE 25°–30°

GENERAL USE 30°–40°

Figure 130.

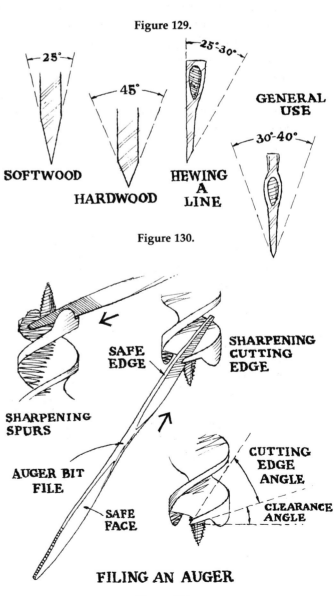

SHARPENING SPURS

SAFE EDGE

SHARPENING CUTTING EDGE

AUGER BIT FILE

SAFE FACE

CUTTING EDGE ANGLE

CLEARANCE ANGLE

FILING AN AUGER

Figure 131.

Handsaw sharpening requires several steps. First, the blade must be "joined"; that is, the points of teeth along the cutting edge must be made even or all the same height by running a file along them (Fig. 132). This needs to be done only every third or fourth filing. Next, individual teeth must be "set" with a special tool called a saw set (Fig. 133). Alternate teeth are bent slightly, either to the right or left side of the blade. Thus, the saw kerf or cut is wider than the thickness of the saw blade, and this clearance prevents the saw from binding against the wood and pulling with difficulty. Hard, dry wood requires saw teeth with less set than soft, wet or "green" wood.

Filing shapes and points saw teeth so that they may cut wood flawlessly and easily. The edge of a crosscut saw is beveled while teeth of a ripsaw are filed straight across, as shown in Figure 134. When filing the teeth of any saw, stand on one side of the saw and file every other tooth. The saw is then reversed, end for end, and the remaining unfiled teeth are sharpened. The cutting angle of saw teeth must be consistent; a cardboard template, marked with the appropriate filing angle, can help to maintain regularity of the angle being filed.

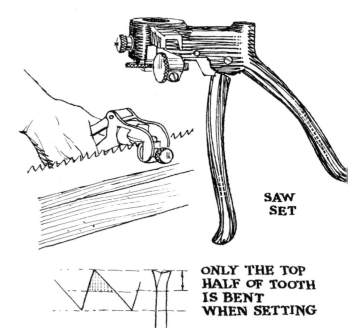

SAW SET

ONLY THE TOP HALF OF TOOTH IS BENT WHEN SETTING

Figure 133.

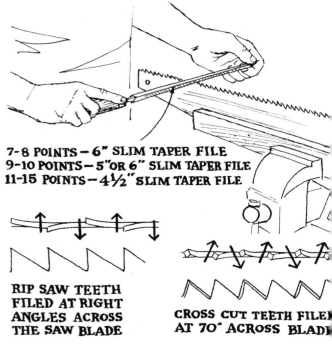

7-8 POINTS – 6" SLIM TAPER FILE
9-10 POINTS – 5" OR 6" SLIM TAPER FILE
11-15 POINTS – 4½" SLIM TAPER FILE

RIP SAW TEETH FILED AT RIGHT ANGLES ACROSS THE SAW BLADE

CROSS CUT TEETH FILE[D] AT 70° ACROSS BLAD[E]

Figure 134.

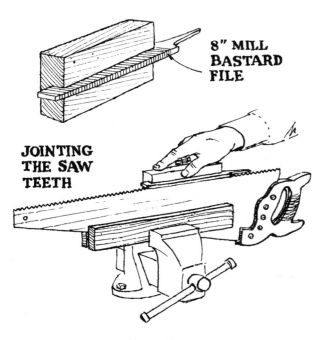

8" MILL BASTARD FILE

JOINTING THE SAW TEETH

Figure 132.

PART II
THE SHOP

Tools were made and
  born were hands,
Every farmer understands.
       William Blake

VIEW OF THE TOOL HOUSE OF TOWNSEND SHARPLESS, AT HIS SUMMER RESIDENCE IN BIRMINGHAM TOWNSHIP, CHESTER COUNTY, PENN.

Chapter 9
PLANNING

It is unfortunate that so many beginning homesteaders have had little or no previous workshop experience. Few novitiates have accumulated the necessary tools or are reasonably familiar with the seven categories of tool use enumerated in a previous section of this book. Perhaps one reason for this regrettable circumstance is that, as children, few had the opportunity to participate in activities or projects taking place in a well-equipped shop managed by a skilled workperson. In these times, it seems that working with one's hands is seldom considered a vital aspect of education or living experience; it is generally assumed more desirable for students to learn to use only their mental processes for achievement in fields more monetarily rewarding than those of the vocational crafts.

Consequently, would-be homesteaders must often begin at "square one" when they seek to acquire the skills of using basic hand tools. To facilitate this process of self-education, the work place should be the very best, a place conducive to "work spirit" or that sense of self that finds joy in achievement through use of one's mind *and* body. In a well-designed, well-equipped, and well-organized work environment, a homesteader may readily discover that hand, tool, and mind can function exceedingly well as a unit for one in pursuit of creative work expression.

The prototype shop described in this book is one we have built for ourselves, a design that has evolved over time from other similar structures (Fig. 136). Its general siting and the organization of its work space dictate its design. It provides us with ample protected storage space for the orderly accumulation of tools and supplies with which to build or improve the homestead. It is also a place in which the reconditioning of equipment and the restoration of tools may be done at any time, especially during inclement weather. Maintenance—that routine servicing of tools and implements to repair or replace worn parts and to periodically lubricate and adjust them—is best done here. For this reason, veteran shopworkers invariably underscore the importance of this aspect of shopwork by calling this homestead structure the "service center."

This center, hub, or core should be either convenient to or centrally located for all parts of the homestead while remaining independent of all other structures. Emphatically stated: It should not be attached to other habitable structures—fire and toxic substances are sometimes associated with shopwork. Because of the hazardous potential of some shop activities, we feel it is imperative to make this building as fireproof as possible.

A warm, southern exposure, adequate drainage, and maximum light and ventilation are other factors important to shop design, for often the homestead workship is used during the darker, wintery months. A quick-fired wood-burning heater is therefore essential on chill

Figure 136. *Completed workshop as viewed from the northwest.*

Figure 137. *The workshop under construction.*

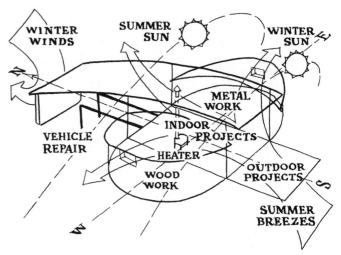

Figure 138. *Models of various workshop designs.*

Figure 139.

days. The shop should be wired for electricity and supplied with running water. Easy access is as essential to the shopworker as it is for the homestead's largest piece of machinery.

Homesteaders pursuing specialized workshop activity, such as woodworking, might choose to redesign the work space and tool arrangement of our prototype shop to accommodate their particular needs and purposes. For example, for one homestead-shop project, with the clients' participation, we constructed a series of scale models (illustrated in Figure 138) in order to properly site and arrange their workshop. Their site sloped abruptly westward toward a streambed, so that it was necessary to locate the workshop at the highest, most-accessible part of their site. They did not want a grease pit for vehicular maintenance, and subdivision covenants required that both house and shop blend architecturally.

Work space is organized according to the various functions taking place in each annex: woodworking, metalworking, and automotive repair. A large, unobstructed paved area in the center of the workshop, partially indoors and partially outdoors, is used as a work space in which to build sizable projects or to repair bulky equipment. This area, located at the intersection of the other activity areas, provides the worker with convenient access to all tools and resources of the shop (Fig. 139).

All woodworking and metalworking tools are appropriately stored in their respective, curvilinear work areas, which are designed to facilitate work flow and safe, easy access to various substations within each work area. In the metalworking annex, there are zones for welding, pipe threading, and tool sharpening as well as for general bench use. The arrangement of these areas will be detailed in Part III.

Figure 140. *Curved retaining wall.*

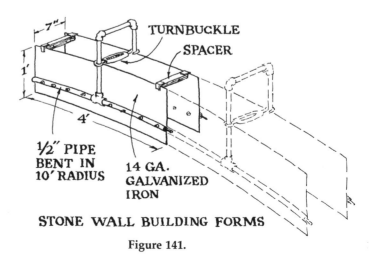

7"

TURNBUCKLE

SPACER

1'

4'

½" PIPE
BENT IN
10' RADIUS

14 GA.
GALVANIZED
IRON

STONE WALL BUILDING FORMS

Figure 141.

Chapter 10
BUILDING

To begin construction of the homestead service center, the first matter to be considered is the finished level of the shop floor. Two factors determine exactly what this level should be: ramps of the vehicular maintenance-and-repair pit must be level with this finished floor, and the floor of the pit should be approxximately 4½ feet below this plane to provide clearance for one to work beneath vehicles. Therefore, for our shop, we first built a 4½-foot-high curved retaining wall, choosing nearby stone as the material for this and all other walls of the project (Fig. 140). We packed stone against the sides of two movable metal forms, filling between and behind each stone with concrete. When both forms were completely full, the first was removed from the masonry and was leap-frogged over the second to an advanced position. In this manner, there was adequate time for each form-load of material to set up or to become somewhat firm. Once these materials had settled, a turnbuckle on the form could be unscrewed to release tension on the packed masonry, allowing the builder to remove the form (Fig. 141). We used stone of an average thickness of 4 inches. With its concrete backing, this curving wall was a total thickness of 7 inches and sufficiently strong to retain 4½ feet of earth.

Since so little concrete was required to build this wall, we found we could mix mortar with relative ease in our manually operated cement mixer (Fig. 142). We devised this mixer by modifying a discarded electric-driven one and found the chore of turning it by hand far more enjoyable than listening to the incessant drone of a laboring engine. We also benefited by the healthy, rhythmical physical exercise involved in this task.

Ramps for our repair pit were salvaged from the metal channel of an old truck frame. This elevated rack (Fig. 143) makes possible the easy, consistent performance of preventive maintenance on homestead vehicles, from under-chassis greasing and adjustments to changing oil. Certain types of motor repair are also more accessible with this arrangement; piston rods, for example, may be loosened from beneath an engine as one stands erect, working in ample light and ventilation.

When the depth of the repair pit (or the height of its ramp) has been ascertained, the level of the shop floor is known. The next order of construction is to set or position all upright pipes that support roof beams relative to their prescribed height above shop-floor level. A shoe plate is welded to the bottom of each of these pipes (Fig. 144) and their top end is pre-drilled to receive the two ⅝-inch-thick bolts that fasten roof beams to them (Fig. 145). These roof supports are then set *absolutely plumb* in an 8-inch-round concrete pier poured to a depth below maximum frost penetration (Fig. 146). Other pipe supports located in the shop's interior need only be sunk in a 12-inch-square concrete pad that is a foot deep and bears on firm soil. We used 2-inch iron pipes for these supports, the minimum size adequate to support the shop roof.

Figure 142.
Hand-powered cement mixer.

Figure 144. *Steel plates welded to bottom of pipe supports, and chart showing relative strength and stiffness of pipes as supports.*

SHAPE OF SECTION	●	○	▲	■	□	I
	100	637	70	88	341	9.9

RELATIVE STIFFNESS (DEFORMATION RESISTANCE)

	100	332	62	74	280	22.2

RELATIVE STRENGTH (STRESS RESISTANCE)

COMPARISON OF THE
TORSIONAL EFFICIENCIES
OF DIFFERENT SECTIONS
OF EQUAL AREA

(FROM TRANSACTIONS A. S. C. E. VOL. 101 p. 857)

Figure 143. *Elevated grease rack in place.*

Figure 145. *Roof beams bolted to pipe supports.*

Two of the pipe supports located inside the shop are designated as the radius points from which both of the formed exterior walls are swung. Before you begin the forming process, scribe wall locations in chalk by swinging a line from this radius point. A 12-inch-square trench is then dug along this chalked line and is half-filled with gravel or small stone rubble to provide drainage as well as bearing for the masonry walls that will rise above this fill.

Although we chose to build walls of stone, we also suggest two alternative low-cost fireproof wall materials that may be more readily available in some areas. These are stabilized clay and concrete. (Their construction will be discussed in the following chapter.) In either case, wall thicknesses remain 7 inches. Inside the shop, these walls are finished flush with support pipe, which may be drilled to anchor benches and shelves to the walls (Fig. 149).

Figure 146. *Digging holes for roof supports.*

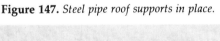

Figure 147. *Steel pipe roof supports in place.*

Where these curved masonry shop walls terminate, a framework is first erected—to become door jambs for the completed structure. Side jambs of this framework are 2 x 4s nailed to a double header built of paired roof beams (Fig. 150). Nails are driven partially into the side of these uprights which, in time, will butt against layers of the masonry wall as it is formed. This framework is then treated with creosote and raised to position where it is carefully plumbed and braced. If a full length of 2 x 2 board is glue-nailed in a curve between the paired roof beams (the header), a rudimentary truss is formed, making it possible to use wood of lesser dimension or 1 x 8 rough-sawn in place of 2 x 8 wood. In addition, prior to construction, roof beams are bolted to pipe supports and sheathing is applied over the project area roof beams, providing either welcome shade or protection from weather.

Figure 148. *Setting perimeter points from radius.*

Figure 149. *View of interior wall showing pipe flush with wall.*

1X8 BEAM

2X4 SUPPORT

DOOR FRAMEWORK BUILT ON GROUND

2X4 SUPPORT

FRAMEWORK IN PLACE

2X2 STIFFENER GLUE~NAILED BETWEEN 1X8 BEAMS

2X4 UPRIGHT SUPPORT

PROTRUDING NAILS

PLAN DETAIL

12 X 12 TRENCH

6" GRAVEL FILL

"H" ANCHOR

CONCRETE PIER

Figure 150.
Construction and placement of stiffened door header.

Figure 151. *An owner-built shop under construction.*

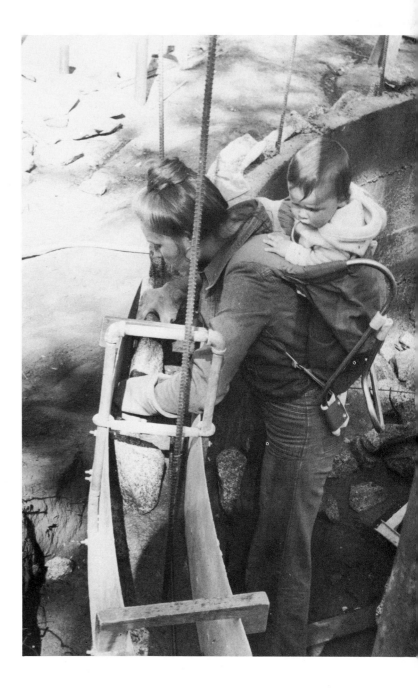

Masonry walls of this workshop are formed by the same simple process used to build the retaining wall of the repair pit, a task that can be done rapidly and with ease by even the most inexperienced builder. Recently, on a project familiar to us, the husband of a family supplied concrete and stone while the wife placed this material in wall forms as she carried their infant son on her back. Their delight in their accomplishment is reflected in the quality of the stonework, shown in Figure 151.

Stone may be packed in these movable metal forms in a fraction of the time that it takes to lay up a stone wall by hand—and without having to build the extensive array of heavy wooden forms customarily used for this purpose (Fig. 152). With our form, only one adjustment of the turnbuckle is necessary to secure alignment of the work, yet when completed it appears professionally done. Cement is packed partially around but primarily behind the stone as it is laid against the sides of the form—as much as needed to hold it in place while other stone is added to the form. This method of placement reveals deep, shadowy joints between stones on the face of the wall when the form is removed.

Each course makes a layer of wall a foot high. When this masonry wall is even with the top of the roof beams, the forms must be inclined to adjust to the downward pitch of the roof (Fig. 153). Thus wall and roof may join or intersect. To serve as nailers for roof sheathing, short lengths of *treated* 2 x 2 block are embedded in the fresh concrete of this last layer of wall (Fig. 154). These blocks are securely anchored in the concrete by nails partially driven into the underside of the block. The concrete will bond to the nails as it sets and the block will be firmly held in place.

Figure 152. *Cast walls with movable metal forms.*

Figure 153. *For top layer of stone, the forms must be inclined to adjust to the downward pitch of the roof.*

Figure 154. *Preparations for roof sheathing:*
2 × 2 blocks are embedded in the fresh concrete of the last layer of wall to serve as nailers for the sheathing.

Figure 155. *Preparing a seat for the window sill.*

Figure 156. *Window sill and joint ready to set in wall.*

Figure 157. *Embedding the sill into fresh concrete.*

To build window openings, set a *treated* 2 x 4 sill into a fresh layer of concrete at appropriate height (Figs. 155 and 156). Again, nails should be partially driven into the bottom side of the sill so that it is firmly held in the mortar (Fig. 157). Nails are also partially driven into *treated* 2 x 4 window jambs to make a positive bond with the concrete-and-stone wall formed up against them. These jambs should be plumbed when nailed to the sill and to roof beams (Figs. 158, 159, and 160).

Roof sheathing consists of staggered layers of

Figure 158. *Jamb is anchored to beam.*

Figure 159.

Figure 160. *Completed window frames.*

1-inch rough-sawn boards, which are laid directly across roof beams, exclusive of any roof joists whatsoever (Fig. 161). This double-board lamination makes for a well-braced roof diaphragm, preventing springiness in any part of the roof system. Sheathing boards should, therefore, be as long as possible to span the distance between beams. Twenty-foot lengths are ideal for spanning four bays without waste.

To roof our prototype shop we used sod. We laid 6-mil polyethylene plastic sheeting over 90-pound rolled roofing, and placed 4 inches of sod atop these materials. We are pleased and satisfied with the result. For another type of insulated, fireproof roof, cover a single layer of 90-pound rolled roofing with a 2-inch layer of stabilized clay (Fig. 162). The clay protects the tar paper from deterioration and at the same time fireproofs the exterior surface of the roof. A trim strip of sheet metal is first attached to the edge of the roof to contain the clay. Then plastic mesh is sandwiched between two 1-inch applications of clay (Fig. 163). The formula for this compound is detailed in the following chapter. In time, this surface may lightly slough off, at which time it could be restabilized with a coat of bitumul brushed over the surface. Chevron Chemical Company manufactures a soil stabilizer, called Suferm, which protects the clay roof surface from erosion and weathering by penetrating into the soil to form a hard, durable crust. For particulars, contact Chevron Chemical Company, Sulfur Products Division Box 3744, San Francisco, CA 94119.

Once roofing has been completed, the concrete slab floor of the shop may be cast (Fig.

Figure 161. *Trimming roof sheathing and beam ends.*

Figure 162. *Applying stabilized-clay roof surface.*

Figure 163. *Plastic mesh is sandwiched between two 1-inch applications of clay.*

164). It will slow-cure in the shade of the sheathed roof. A perfectly leveled screed board is laid along both lines of interior pipe supports that carry the roof and separate the work annexes from the central project areas. The annexes are then laid with sandy or gravelly fill to within 1½ inches of the top of the screed boards, and the central work area is laid with fill to within 3 inches of the top of the screed boards on either side of it as well. The center project area is then poured with concrete and finished smooth (Fig. 165). It is advisable to insert metal fabric in the center floor slab for reinforcement, for this part of the shop floor will receive heavy use. On the following day, screed boards are removed and annex slabs are cast. A thinner 1½-inch cast is permissible in the annexes where

only foot traffic is borne and where the greater portion of the area is taken up with benches, cabinets, and lightweight machinery and tools.

Finally, install windows and doors. All glazing in our shop is translucent sheet fiberglass, for a view to the outside through these high windows is superfluous. In the summer, hinged windows are fastened to the ceiling for maximum ventilation and light. Doors, too, may be swung open, out of the way of shop activities. Benches and storage cabinets, tool racks, and bins are built next. Finally, tools, equipment, and spare parts are organized in preparation for the many years of productive, satisfying work that will take place in this homestead service center.

Figure 164. *Preparing the ground for floor slab.*

Figure 165. *Finishing the slab of the central section.*

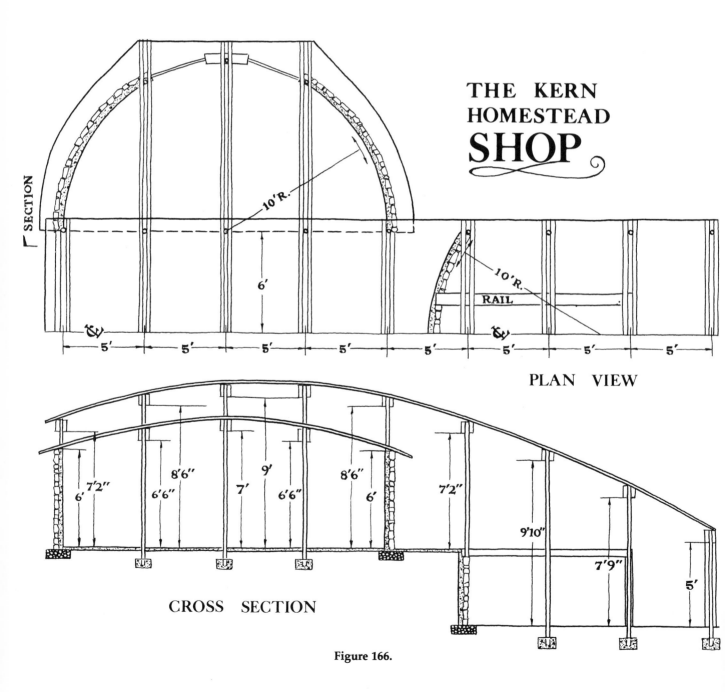

SECTION

10'R.

6'

5' 5' 5' 5' 5' 5' 5' 5'

10'R.

RAIL

PLAN VIEW

THE KERN HOMESTEAD SHOP

6' 7'2" 8'6" 7' 9' 6'6" 8'6" 6' 7'2" 9'10" 7'9" 5'
6'6"

CROSS SECTION

Figure 166.

Chapter 11
ALTERNATIVE WALL MATERIALS

When readily found, stone is a practical material with which to build the exterior walls of a homestead building. It is, however, by no means the only or even the best material for wall building. We used stone to build the walls of our homestead service center because its source was nearby, and we are particularly attracted to building with this natural material.

Homesteaders who have deposits of clay on their property are as fortunate as those with stone outcroppings, creek sandbeds, gravel pits, or certain kinds of soils. All of these materials may be used for wall building. By adding a small quantity of stabilizer (or binder), clay, stone, soil, or sand and gravel (cement) can be used to make strong, fireproof, rotproof, inexpensive walls. To utilize these materials, we have designed several forming devices that are easy to build and to use. They take the back-breaking labor out of the building process and eliminate the need for the owner-builder to have had previous technical building experience.

Soil stabilization makes it possible to utilize a wide range of soils for building purposes, and stabilization may be done on the construction site, a factor contributing to the low cost of earthen walls. One method of soil stabilization is called rammed-earth construction, a procedure by which soil is mechanically compacted. With this process, soil strength increases as voids in soil structure and permeability decrease. Its greatest strength is reached when fine particles fill the spaces between coarser soil particles. Added to a soil-cement mix, moisture is the critical factor. Small amounts will displace the air in soil and help fine-grained particles to consolidate around larger particles. Too much water, however, will tend to occupy soil spaces that would otherwise fill with solids. When the water eventually evaporates, these pockets fill with air. This type of earthen-wall construction requires well-built heavy forms that will withstand the pressure of forceful tamping. The labor factor in this building system is excessive.

Clay, on the other hand, has some exciting possibilities as a building material. A soil substance found virtually everywhere, it is often concealed beneath layers of topsoil. It is more apparent in arid regions where, due to wind erosion, it may be found closer to the surface. In other areas, clay outcroppings may be discovered where the earth has been cut through, as in creek or river beds or along roadways and railroad embankments. They are identified by their crumbly, irregular, exposed faces.

If, when a small amount of soil sample is mixed with water a plastic sticky mass results, you can be reasonably certain that the soil sample contains clay. Color is not a reliable indicator, for clay can be red, green, gray, tan, brown, or white, depending on its iron-oxide content or its carbonaceous matter. Iron oxide, for example, gives red clay its characteristic hue. Most clays contain about 5 percent iron oxide; with any less, clay is said to be white.

Weathering and structural properties of clay may be improved without resorting to high-temperature firing, such as that given brick. Clay may be stabilized by adding organic and inorganic substances, which bind and waterproof clay particles to produce a strong, durable soil wall. Resinous and bituminous compounds are the organic stabilizers commonly used in this process. They waterproof soil particles and behave like glue, contributing to the cohesive strength of the mass. This method of soil-wall building requires less labor to erect than compacted-soil walls.

Bitumen is the general term used to designate any of several hard or semisolid materials obtained as asphaltic residue in the distillation of coal tar, wood tar, petroleum, or occurring as natural asphalt. To combine with soil, a bituminous material must first be mixed with water. As an emulsion, asphalt is suspended as fine globules in water. When mixed with soil, these asphaltic globules adhere to the surface of soil particles. When dried, the compound is solid and impervious to moisture.

There are fifteen commonly used grades of emulsified asphalt. For best results when building walls, it is important to select the proper grade of this material. Some grades are medium-setting (coded *MS* and *CMS*) while others are slow-setting (coded *SS* and *CSS*). "Slow-setting" means that the emulsion slowly separates back into asphalt and water, leaving a film of asphalt on the grains of soil—the hallmark of the stabilizing process. A slow-setting, also called slow-breaking, emulsion is preferable because it separates only after being thoroughly mixed with soil. The Asphalt Emulsion Association is a manufacturers' organization that has recently been formed to promote use of this material. It has published a book entitled *Emulsion Plants in the United States,* a reference work helpful to those wishing to locate a source of asphalt stabilizer in their area. You can write to this association at 1000 Vermont Ave. NW, Washington, DC 20005. Ask them for the plant nearest you that produces *CSS-1.*

Hydrated lime, an inorganic soil stabilizer, can be used alone or in combination with emul-sified asphalt to stabilize soil. It forms when quicklime reacts with water, a process called "slaking." When added to clay and compacted, lime cements soil crystals; that is, metallic soil ions carrying a weak electrical charge are readily replaced by the calcium ions in lime, which carry a stronger charge. Thus, soil particles are bound together in a rigid mass. The more clay there is in soil, the more effective lime is as a stabilizing agent. Highway engineers have long specified lime to increase the load-carrying capacity of soils abundant in clay. In 1960, the U.S. Highway Research Board investigated lime-stabilized clay soils. Generally, they found that 6 to 8 percent lime was an optimum amount with which to effectively stabilize clay (as illustrated by the chart in Figure 167).

The final component of a stabilized-clay wall is an organic binder, any natural material like chopped straw or pine needles. Prehistoric wall builders knew the structural value of straw or reeds added to clay—pre-Columbian potters reinforced clay pots with the fuzz from cattails. Organic matter increases the dry strength of clay, for the embedded fibers increase tensile strength. Fibers also aid the evaporation of moisture from inner wall space, allowing the even, consistent drying of wall interiors and distributing the forces of expansion and contraction.

Preparing stabilized clay for use as wall material is a relatively simple procedure. First, build a mixing trough (illustrated in Figure 168) by framing a 4 x 8 sheet of plywood with 2 x 6 side boards. Spread 100 shovelfuls of clay in this trough and add 6 shovelfuls of hydrated lime. Mix these briefly with a hoe. Then add 20 gallons of water and 5 gallons of CSS emusified asphalt. Mix these together thoroughly with the hoe. Finally, slowly add an equivalent of 100 shovelfuls of chopped straw while mixing the entire contents with the hoe. As the last portion of straw is added, the compound becomes stiff and difficult to work. At this stage, we usually work the mass with bare feet (as the small boy is doing) to mix it thoroughly (Fig. 168). The proportion we found best is 7 clay, 7 chopped straw, 4 water, 1 asphalt emulsion, and 1 hy-

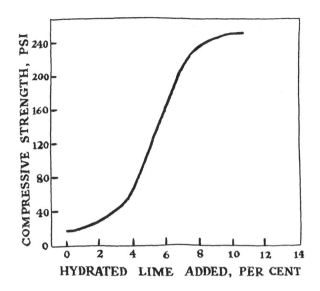

RELATION OF ADDITIONS OF LIME
TO STRENGTH
(FROM U.S. HGWY. BOARD, 1960)

Figure 167.

drated lime (50 shovelfuls each of clay and straw, 20 gallons of water and 5 of asphalt, and 7 shovelfuls of lime).

The same forming system used to build packed-stone walls is also used to build stabilized-clay walls (Fig. 169). As this material is shoveled into the form, it is packed in place with a wooden tamper. Then, as one form sets, another is filled with stabilized clay. This allows sufficient time for an initial firming of the mixture before the form is removed. An end gate on the leading form contains the material in the mold. A 6-inch-thick reinforced concrete bond course must be poured at the foot and the top of the wall to tie the earth-wall material, the pipe supports, and the bond beams together as a unified construction. Adding to its strength, the curve of this wall also makes this unor-

Figure 168. *Mixing in the last portion of straw in preparing stabilized clay.*

Figure 169. *After stabilized clay is shoveled into the form, it is packed in place with a wooden tamper.*

thodox building method structurally viable.

In *The Owner-Built Homestead* (Charles Scribner's Sons, 1977), we related how the curved slip form could be used to build all homestead structures: raised garden beds, a root cellar, an all-masonry wood-fueled heater/cookstove, a workshop, a privy/greenhouse, a bathhouse, a water tank, a fish pond, and the homestead house. Any one of these curvilinear walls swings from a radius point, eliminating the need for building expensive heavy wooden forms. Since we wrote that book, we have built a number of these structures, experimenting each time with the quantity of material that could be used without sacrificing the strength or structural integrity of our buildings. We now build concrete walls 1½ inches thick, using a single form to build every structure on the homestead by simply adjusting a couple of turnbuckles. The same slip form will build a 50-foot-diameter fish pond or a 3-foot-diameter masonry stove. Single-wall thickness or double-wall thickness may be built, the latter with an inner air cavity that may be insulated.

Using the double-wall slip form is perhaps the easiest, fastest, and least expensive way to build walls. This form is swung from a radius rod, scribing the perimeter of a building. With each revolution, a layer of wall 4 inches high is cast. The concrete mix is six parts pea gravel and sand, mixed half and half, combined with one part cement; this is mixed fairly dry. It is placed in the metal form with a trowel, and the form is slid forward immediately when full. The first and last courses, each containing two ⅜-inch reinforcing rods, are poured solid; there is no air cavity in this course. However, between these top and bottom courses, double walls are formed, each 1½ inches thick and separated by a 4-inch cavity. At frequent intervals, these walls are joined with heavy wire ties. The cavity may be filled with sawdust, an effective inexpensive insulation. To discourage insect infestation of this insulation, add a shovelful of lime (dry) to each cement mixer full of dry sawdust. Churn this mixture for several revolutions and then shovel it into the wall cavity.

Whether stone, earth, or concrete is used to build shop walls, the basic structural system remains the same. Two-inch steel pipes are first set in concrete piers, which extend from below frost level up to within 6 inches of the finished floor level. A 12-inch-square trench is then dug around the perimeter of the building, the top of the trench being flush with the level of the floor. In this ditch, place a 6-inch layer of crushed rock or fist-sized stone rubble. Level it with the top of the pipe-support pier. A reinforced concrete bond beam, carrying two rows of ⅜-inch steel bars, is then cast on top of the gravel fill. This bond beam is the same width as the finished wall above it—or 7 inches wide. It is 6 inches deep, whereas the concrete slip form is but 4 inches high.

The finished wall is formed and topped with another bond course of reinforced concrete. This final course also contains treated nailer blocks to which roof sheathing will later be attached.

Figure 170. *A finished workshop with walls made of stabilized clay with slip-formed walls of concrete.*

Figure 171. *Two more views of the finished workshop.* Bottom photo by Michael Eckerman.

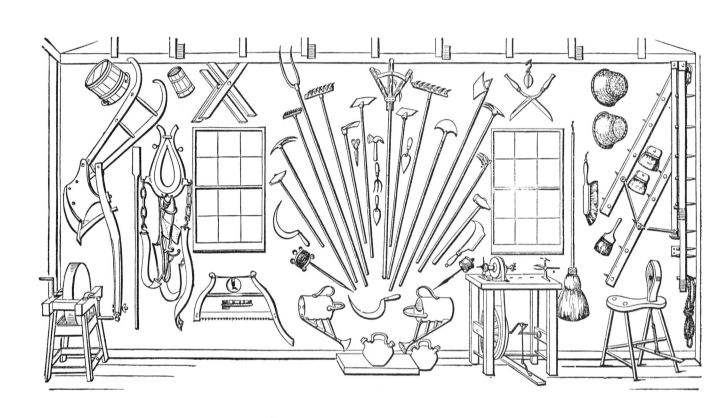

PART III
THE TOOLS IN THE SHOP

All ranged in order, and disposed
  with grace,
Shape marked of each, and each one
  in its place;
Nor this alone the curious eye to
  please,
But to be found, whene'er required
  with ease.
If used or loaned, and not returned
  by rule,
The vacant shape will show the
  missing tool;
Thus often the careless will
  improve,
And rules of order soon will learn
  to love.

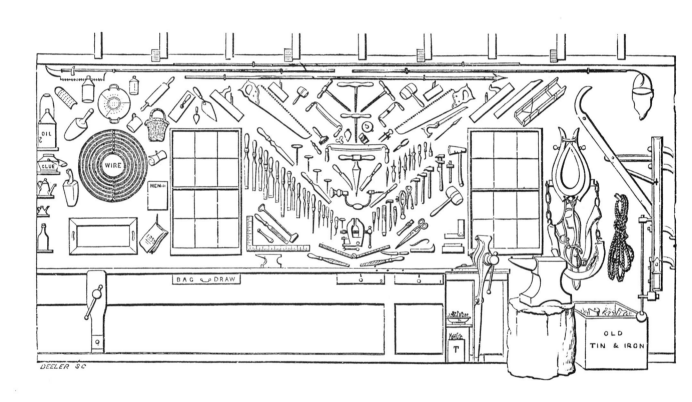

OIL

GLUE

WIRE

MEM

BAG DRAW

OLD
TIN & IRON

DEELER SC

Chapter 12

ORGANIZATION AND MANAGEMENT OF THE HOMESTEAD WORKSHOP

In Philadelphia, 1862, some 200 farm tools and implements were hung on the walls of a 12-by-20 shop building in the manner described by the anonymous author of the preceding poem. This organization of tools so impressed editors of *The American Agriculturalist* magazine that they documented the layout in one of their monthly issues that year. The article (reprinted in 1975 in *The Compleat Farmer*, Universe Books, New York) mentions that iron hooks and staples, "of a size proportional to the weight of the tool," anchored many tools and devices to walls so that they could be removed or replaced with rapidity and ease. This, too, may well have been the first instance in which the outline of each tool was traced upon the wall where it hung so that "the vacant shape will show the missing tool." Today, this practice is called tool silhouetting, a procedure we use to place all wall-hung tools in our contemporary shop.

In the first part of this book, we wrote of the various tools used in the homestead workshop, followed by a section giving construction details for a building that can safely and conveniently house this equipment and provide sheltered work space for the manufacture or repair of homestead articles. With this section of our book, we bring tools and workshop together, suggesting the best organization of tools for their appropriate use in various activity centers.

In each work center, tool organization is determined by frequency of use. All implements and supplies regularly employed in specific work activities should be placed on a nearby wall-hung rack. Those that are seldom used should be kept in a drawer or on a shelf. Since several work projects may proceed simultaneously in any work center, tools should be arranged so they can be used interchangeably between tasks.

Thought should be given to tool acquisition. Before any purchase, a homesteader must learn a tool's limitations, as well as its capacities and best uses. In essence, the task itself dictates which tool should be used, each tool being best adapted for a specific use.

Shopworkers tend to accumulate more tools than necessary when they organize their first shop. Purchase should be made only at the time a tool is most needed, and the tool should be of a size and quality that will serve both its present and future use. A homesteader should consider whether any saving that accrues from a "bargain" purchase really justifies that tool's choice. Tool selection must correspond to one's skill with its use and to the frequency with which it will be employed in various workshop projects.

Tools should be acquired on the basis of worker safety as well. A cheap hammer, for instance, will likely be made with a cast-iron head. When struck with a glancing blow, this tool can fling chips of metal toward the eyes. Buy, instead, a hammer with a head made of steel alloy, one that is drop forged or metal hammered when hot. Edge tools—like saws, chisels, or planes—should be of the very best quality. Saws of poor quality will not retain their set or tooth adjustment, causing irritating delays in accomplishing tasks.

The novice shopworker should always buy tools from a reputable supplier: a local hardware store or a large department store, like Sears or Wards, which have a reliable return policy for most of their products. By "shopping around," one has the opportunity to compare the quality and heft of several brands. The Craftsman brand of tools sold by Sears is generally an excellent choice. Mail-order-tool purchase can be disappointing for those unfamiliar with tool and brand names. However, suppliers like U.S. General (100 Commercial Street, Plainview, NY 11803) sell many quality hand and power tools at discount prices. Carefully read the description of a tool in the access catalog before ordering.

Many tools, like socket-wrench sets, are cheaper when bought as a complete unit with carrying case. Several sets of inexpensive screwdrivers and vise grip pliers can be dispersed to various work centers within the shop. This convenience is well worth the duplication of these tools.

Generally speaking, our shop has another feature in common with the model shop of 1862; no loose objects are allowed to scatter over the shop floor or beneath counters or workbenches. (When our demonstration workshop was photographed, however, some tool arrangements were in a state of flux and in some illustrations do not conform to this prescription.) When properly arranged, the entire floor area, which should be swept frequently to reduce fire hazard and careless accident, may be quickly cleaned by a bristle push broom. A tidy floor and uncluttered counters are important morale boosters when beginning a work project in the homestead shop.

Chapter 13
METALWORKING

Homestead shop arrangement might best be "shown" to the newcomer by simply "walking through" the building while we indicate various tool and activity centers and give our reasons for organizing them as we have. Following the diagram of the layout on the next page you can see that the shop has four main working sections: metalworking with metalworking supplies, a central project area, a vehicular repair pit with a place for parts and supplies, and a woodworking area containing woodworking supplies. (A separate chapter will be devoted to each of these.)

Our workshop is entered through a 4-foot-wide access door which opens to the south side of the building. This door, unlocked by key from the outside, has a deadbolt lock, which is the most reliable device for securing any entranceway. When one wishes to go out through the closed (and thus locked) door, turning a knob releases the bolt on this clasp.

A series of coat hooks are attached at head height to the inner surface of the access door. The cotton apron, mentioned in Chapter 3, hangs here. A mechanic's skullcap, worn primarily when working beneath greasy vehicles or when welding, hangs from a hook on this door, as does a pair of leather working gloves. The gloves are useful when handling hot or slippery metal or when welding, but are seldom used for general shopwork. Gloves interfere with close, sensitive contact with tools.

Having entered the shop, you will notice a 30-gallon trash barrel beside the door for disposing of all noncombustible wastes. Combustible wastes are incinerated in the centrally located heater stove. Fastened to the wall above the trash barrel (W1) are two items commonly used on the homestead: a 4-foot length of gasoline siphon hose and a pair of battery jumper cables. A fire extinguisher and a flashlight are adjacent to the entry door for ready use.

A 3-foot-long, 2-foot-wide maintenance bench (B1) is installed between the trash barrel and shop sink, a well-lighted space for tool sharpening and parts cleaning (Fig. 173, position ⚠). Here we keep both fine and coarse Carborundum stones and grinding oil. A foot-powered grindstone is stored beneath this bench. Cleaning solvents and penetrating oils are stocked on a shelf above this work counter (TS1). On the wall between the counter and this storage shelf (W2) hang wire and fiber brushes, putty knives, and metal scrapers for cleaning parts and reconditioning tools. Also on this section of wall are utility brackets that support various types of grease guns and tire-changing tools—tire irons, lug wrench, hydraulic hand jack and air pump, a tire-bead breaker, and a hot-patch clamp. A three-tiered set of compartments above the counter (C1) contains tools and spare parts for work on three major vehicular maintenance systems: electrical, tire, and battery. Each of these compartments contains the following:

ELECTRICAL

- spare fuses
- feeler gauge
- spark-plug gapper
- ignition wrench set
- ignition point file
- spare light bulbs
- spark-plug wrench

BATTERY

- post and terminal cleaner
- battery terminal pliers
- hydrometer
- terminal puller
- battery carrier
- spare battery terminals

TIRE

- air pressure gauge
- tubeless tire repair kit
- hot patches
- valve tool
- spare valve cores

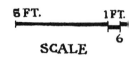

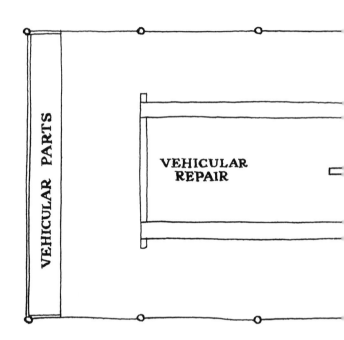

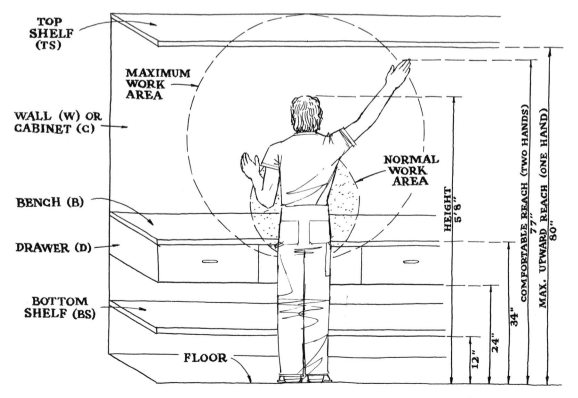

Figure 172.

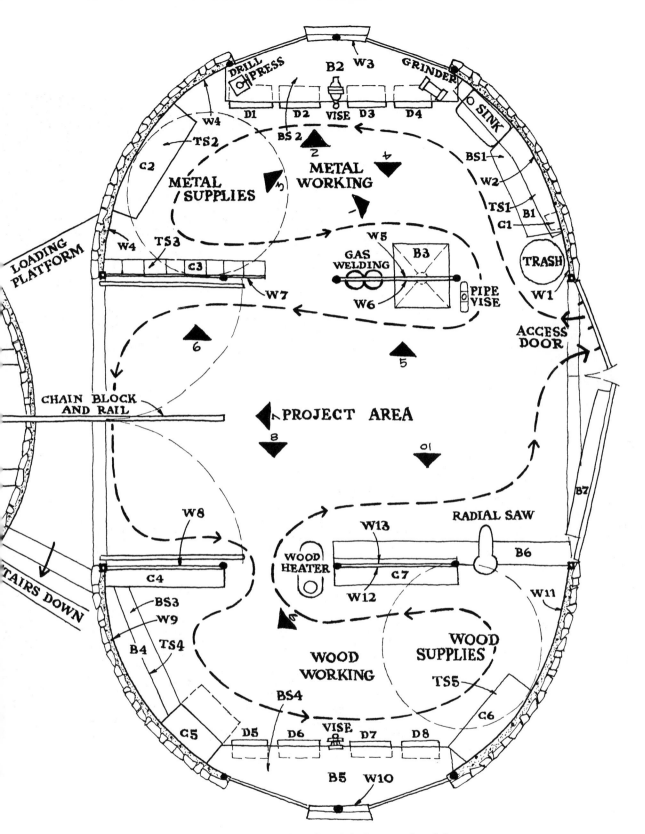

Figure 173. *Floor plan of the homestead workshop.*

Figure 174. *The maintenance bench—a well-lighted space for tool sharpening and parts cleaning.*
Photo by Michael Eckerman

A shelf below this counter (BS1) stores 5-gallon containers of motor oil and transmission grease. On the shelf above (TS1), smaller 2-gallon containers of used oil, bearing grease, transmission fluid, and antifreeze are stored, along with an assortment of funnels and oil and grease dispensers. Cleaning pans for parts are also found here. The shelf is 7 feet long, ample for the wide assortment of little-used liquid and semiliquid materials involved in vehicular maintenance and shop management—like starting fluid, penetrating oil, water-pump grease, hydraulic-jack fluid, and brake fluid. Gasoline is the only liquid stored outside the shop. However, a small gallon can of gasoline-oil mixture, used to fuel 2-cycle engines, is stored inside the shop—far from the welding center or the wood-fired heater stove.

The principle feature of the metalworking annex is its 11-foot-long bench (B2 and Fig. 173, position △); its center is a 5-inch swivel-base machinist's vise. Often shop experts will locate this vise on a separate stand so that the top of its jaws are level with a worker's knuckles, a height conducive to erect working posture. If our workbench were lowered to accommodate this purpose, it would be too low for other work activities. We therefore have compromised bench height, making it a few inches lower than usual so that the vise jaws are more within the normal range of erect working posture. We feel it is more important to us that the vise is located close to metalworking tools, outweighing any disadvantage from its slight increase in height.

When this bench is in use, tools are positioned at three locations, depending on their frequency of use. Those most often used are silhouetted against the wall (W3), those used only occasionally are placed in drawers directly beneath the bench (D1, D2, D3, D4), and those used infrequently are stored in containers on a shelf below the drawers (BS2). Thus wall clutter is avoided. To illustrate: a part is gripped in the vise as one prepares to tighten a nut with an open-end box wrench. Nearby on the wall (W3) to the right hangs a complete set of box wrenches—from 1½-inch to ⅜-inch size in ¹⁄₁₆-

Figure 175. *The 11-foot-long metalworking bench with a 5-inch swivel-base machinist's vise in the center.* Photo by Michael Eckerman

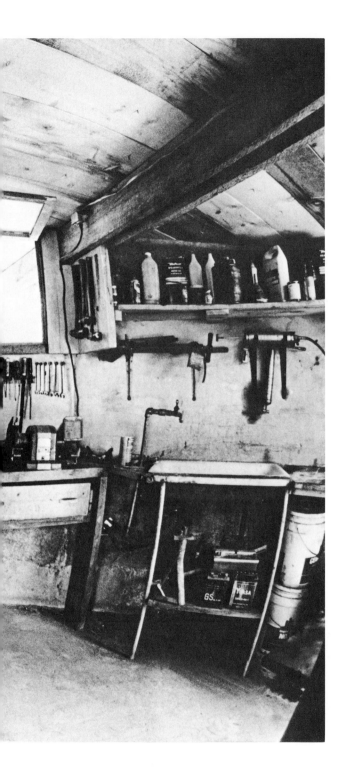

inch increments. Tightening the nut properly sometimes requires more leverage or a special fitting with which to grasp it securely. Therefore, one reaches for a socket wrench stored in a drawer to the left of the vise (D2). On rare occasions, exact tension is required to tighten a nut on a particular automotive part. In a metal chest on the shelf below the bench (BS2) is found an assortment of vehicular overhaul tools, among which is a torque wrench used for such occasions. This tool is not hung on the wall nor is it placed in a drawer, for a year may elapse before it is needed again.

Another example of priority tool location is revealed when using measuring tools while standing at the vise. A box tape, found on the wall behind the vise (W3), accomplishes 90 percent of all metalworking measurement chores. When more accuracy is required, we use a tool—a caliper rule—stored in a drawer (D3) to the right of the vise. This tool registers measurements requiring a high degree of accuracy. For other refinements of measurement, such as checking roundness of the journals of a crankshaft (maybe once a year or less often), we use a micrometer. We don't even include a micrometer set (BS2) in our primary listing of tools, for this is a precision tool more often used by professional machinists.

From the power grinder on the right-hand side to the drill press on the left, the tools silhouetted against the wall behind the metalworking bench (W3) are

- set of three ball peen hammers: 8 oz., 1 lb., 2 lb.; cross-peen, soft-face hammer
- file rack: 10-inch single-cut mill (bastard, second-cut, and smooth); file card, 10-inch single-cut flat, round
- open-end box-wrench set: from ⅜ inch to 1½ inch in ¹⁄₁₆-inch increments
- hand drill, breast drill
- utility knife
- two hacksaws, one with 14 and another with 24 teeth
- chisel-and-punch rack: center punch, prick punch, pin punch, solid punch, set of four cold chisels

- adjustable wrenches: 18 inch, 12 inch, 8 inch, 4 inch
- screwdriver rack: Phillips set, regular set, offset
- 12-inch tin snips, aviation snips
- pliers rack: Bernard, channel locks, vise grip pliers (7½ inch, 10 inch) solid joint pliers
- drill-press vise

The four drawers (D1, D2, D3, D4), which slide out from beneath the bench, are 30 inches wide and 8 inches deep. Each includes a shallow tray for small items. Soldering and electrical repair tools are kept in the right-hand drawer (D4), below the all-purpose grinder. Other fastening tools, like a pop-rivet gun and a hand stapler, are likewise found in this drawer, as are spring clamps, rivet set, flaring tool, electrician's pliers, black and rubber tape, leather punch, and soldering tools. These are itemized in Chapter 7.

Found next to this drawer of fastening tools, to the right of the vise (D3), is a drawer containing an assortment of metalworking tools, including duplicates and those used less frequently than wall-mounted ones. In the tray of this drawer, we keep precision measuring tools, such as a slide caliper, inside and outside caliper, dividers, a wire and thickness gauge, and sharpening templates.

The drawer to the left of the vise (D2) contains two socket-wrench sets: a ½-inch-square driver and a ¼-inch-square drive set. Spare open-end wrenches and an eleven open-end metric wrench set (6–17 mm) are found here. Below the drill press in drawer D1 is our miscellaneous collection of twist drills, reamers, tap-and-die sets (¼ inch to ½ inch by ¹⁄₁₆-inch increments, both USS and SAE), and extractors. Hand-powered tools, like the all-purpose grinder and various drills, are stored on the shelf below the drawers (BS2). This open shelf also holds a box of vehicular repair tools, to be itemized in Chapter 19.

Chapter 14
METALWORKING SUPPLIES

Part of the function of a homestead shop is to provide a suitable place for using and storing tools and equipment. Another equally important function is to provide storage space for materials and supplies. A shopworker is in constant need of bolts and washers, pipe fittings and odd pieces of metal. There are literally hundreds of different hardware items for metalworking that must somehow be categorized and organized. Any item that is misplaced is for all intents and purposes lost, for it is simply unavailable when needed.

Many time-consuming trips to the hardware store can be avoided by stocking essential items and by knowing where they are stored at all times. In this category are spare machine parts and materials. One should have an extra pulley belt for each piece of homestead equipment using one. The investment cost is insignificant when compared to "break-down time" or the expense of a trip to town for the singular purpose of purchasing a pulley belt. Whenever possible buy supplies in gross or bulk lots; this includes petroleum products as well. We cannot imagine a homestead shopowner purchasing a mere half dozen quater-inch stove bolts for a specific project. A quarter-inch stove bolt, whatever its length, is the most common fastener used on the homestead. If six are momentarily needed, buy a box of 100 for eventually they will be used.

The argument for stocking quantities of a wide selection of hardware items goes beyond that of mere convenience. If a part is unavailable or you are unaware of its existence, the temptation is to use an inappropriate substitute. Conversely, when two pieces of metal must be fastened with a bolt, if all alternative bolting methods are known and our shop is stocked with a variety of bolt fasteners, then we can readily choose that which is best for the job. Perhaps we merely wish to drill and tap one of these pieces of metal to insert a set screw or to tap both pieces of metal in order to hold them together with a machine screw. Or perhaps we may choose to drill both pieces, bolting them together with a machine screw and a nut. For a stronger connection, metal may be drilled and tapped and fitted with a cap screw or be drilled and bolted with a machine bolt. Finally, to maximize holding power, we may use a hardened bolt. With knowledge of the alternatives available to us, we can achieve the best results. Seldom does the average homesteader know, for example, that hardened bolts are available and that they may be identified by a coded notch on the head of the bolt (Fig. 176).

In our prototype shop, we have reserved a section of the metalworking alcove for the storage of supplies (Fig. 177, position A). In this area are two built-in units: a bin for large parts (C2) and a cabinet for small parts (C3). In this area, the storage of items is determined merely by their size. A small bolt fits in one of the cabinet compartments but a large pipe fitting requires space in the bin. On the wall between these two

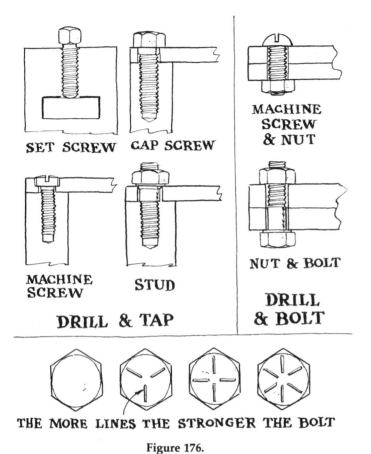

SET SCREW   CAP SCREW   MACHINE SCREW & NUT

MACHINE SCREW   STUD   NUT & BOLT

DRILL & TAP   DRILL & BOLT

THE MORE LINES THE STRONGER THE BOLT

Figure 176.

units (W4), we have placed hooks to hold wire, chain, pulley belts, and rope.

The large-parts bin (C2) is a 5-foot-wide floor-to-ceiling series of shelves, divided down the center. On the top shelf (TS2), one finds new spare parts for various homestead vehicles: spark plugs, oil and air filters, fuel pumps, windshield wipers, etc. On the next shelf down are found galvanized pipe fittings: half inch and less on the left side and three-quarter inch and greater on the right side of the shelf. Other shelves contain copper pipe fittings; hose, valve, and faucet fittings; electrical supplies in-

cluding outlet boxes and switches and plugs, pulleys and bearings, pieces of chain, swivels and hooks, and short lengths of rope. The lowest bin is undivided and contains various kinds of metal scrap, from angle iron to iron rod.

Any piece of iron over 5 feet in length is stored outside the shop in a so-called boneyard. Before starting a metalworking project, we poke around in this area to find essential iron with which to build something new or to repair something old. Any shop that fails to have a well-stocked boneyard is poorly equipped. It may include angle iron from bed frames, old

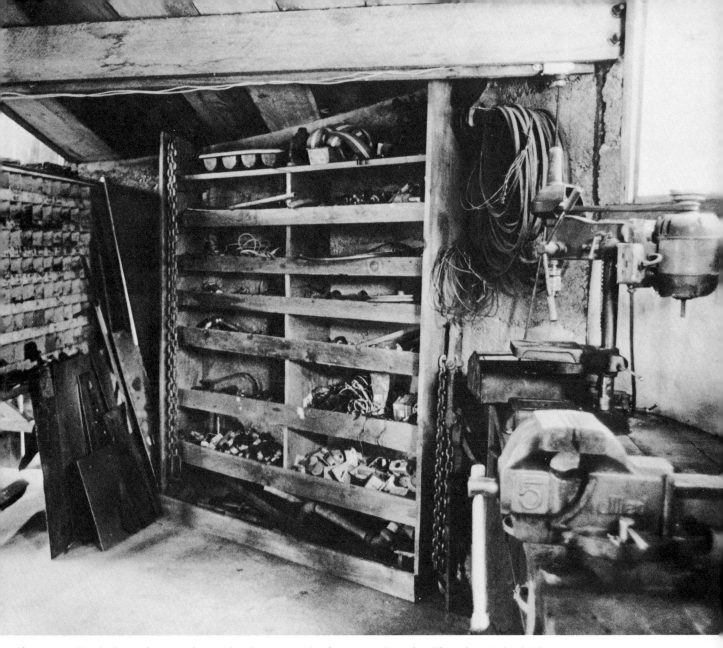

Figure 177. *Two built-in cabinets in the metalworking section for the storage of supplies.* Photo by Michael Eckerman

pipe and metal rods, iron wheels, and lengths of flat steel and sheet iron. No metal object on the homestead should ever be discarded. Rather, pile it up in this scrap yard for future use.

The small-parts cabinet (C3) is compartmentalized both horizontally (to accommodate a variety of hardware) and vertically according to size. The cabinet has numerous cubicles running six vertically and sixteen horizontally. In addition to the many sizes, lengths, and types of bolts, it also holds the following: washers—large, small, fiber, and lock; brass fittings; lead anchors; steel bolts; set screws; rivets; screw eyes; ball bearings; cotter pins; turnbuckles and sheet-metal screws. One compartment contains miscellaneous keys and locks that occasionally match. Longer items, like threaded rod, are stowed on the top shelf (TS3) of the small-parts cabinet.

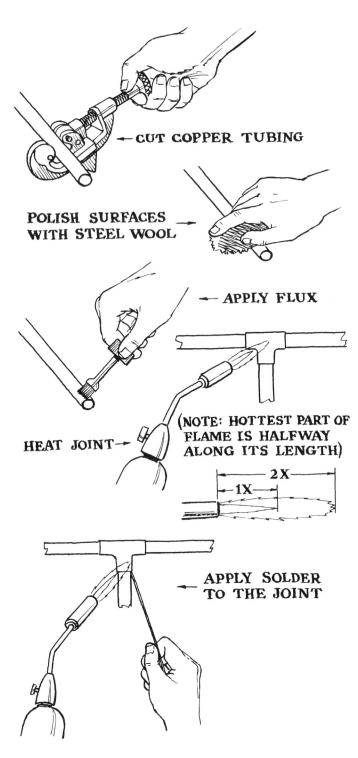

← CUT COPPER TUBING

POLISH SURFACES → WITH STEEL WOOL

→ APPLY FLUX

HEAT JOINT →

(NOTE: HOTTEST PART OF FLAME IS HALFWAY ALONG ITS LENGTH)

2X

1X

APPLY SOLDER → TO THE JOINT

SOLDERING COPPER TUBING

Figure 178.

Chapter 15
SOLDER WELDING

A minimum of knowledge and skill in the art of welding is essential to the performance of metalworking in a homestead shop. When the complete range of welding tools and materials is available, including those for soldering, brazing, and gas welding, one tends to use this method of fastening materials before using others that are more mechanical, for welding is simple, fast, and makes a secure bond.

Two pieces of either like or unlike metal, heated in conjunction with a metal alloy of lower melting point until all three are molten and joined, are said to be "welded." The pieces of metal either joined or actually fused are called the base metal, and the alloy used to join them is called the filler. Depending on the amount of heat necessary to melt the filler, welding is known either as soldering, brazing, or arc welding. Soldering, for example, occurs at a temperature below 800 degrees Fahrenheit, when the heat generated is intense enough to melt the filler but not the base metals. Brazing occurs at temperatures between 800 and 2000 degrees Fahrenheit, where the filler bonds with the base material before it melts. Above this temperature, an arc-welding flame will melt both filler and base metals, fusing them completely.

Whether a shopworker will choose to solder, braze, or arc weld in order to join metals depends on a number of variables, but primarily on the type of base metals to be attached and their thickness. A soldered joint can be impervious to air or water but cannot support either great tensile loading (shear forces) or pressure loading for long periods of time. Soldering is best suited for joining wire, copper pipe fittings, and thin nonferrous metals, like tin, galvanized iron, brass, copper, aluminum, and lead.

All soldering equipment is stored in the bench drawer (D4) across from the metal-welding table (B3). In this drawer, there are three items essential to the performance of quality soldering work: solder, flux, and a heat source.

The Romans may have perfected the art of soldering at expense to their health, for some historians believe that widespread use of toxic lead in filler contributed in some measure to the eventual downfall of Roman civilization. The Romans discovered that by smelting thirty-seven parts of pure lead (which melts at 620 degrees Fahrenheit) with 63 parts of pure tin (which melts at 450 degrees Fahrenheit) an alloy was formed which itself melts at only 360 degrees Fahrenheit—or lower than either of its constituents. However, since tin was rarer and more expensive than lead, they used a 50–50 proportion of lead and tin for their solder, a filler (still in use today) that melted at 415 degrees Fahrenheit. Rarely, except when soldering pewterware, was solder used that was 60 percent tin to 40 percent lead.

In the 2000 years since 50–50 soldering was perfected, numerous changes have occurred in the process. First, a method was found to shape bar solder to form a wire with a hollow core, which could be filled with a flux of either rosin or acid. Flux removes the film of chemical oxide on metal, thereby decreasing surface tension and allowing more direct contact between the solder and the metal. (More about flux later in this chapter.)

Then, it was discovered that silver could substitute for lead in soldering stainless-steel cooking utensils, avoiding any possible lead contamination of foods. Another solder became commercially available for joining sheet aluminum, tubing, and extrusions, and yet another type was found for soldering zinc-based pot metal. Thick, cast metal like pot metal has a high melting point, so certain alloys must be added to its solder, increasing the solder's melting point to as much as 1000 degrees Fahrenheit.

Fluxes, too, are selected on the basis of the types of metal being joined. When flux is heated, it becomes fluid and tends to loosen and lift, or float off, certain chemical impurities, like tarnish and rust, coating the metal. Thus flux enables solder to flow beneath suspended oxides so that the solder may fuse or stick to the metals. When union is complete, surface impurities may be wiped or washed away. Sometimes welders assume that flux alone will entirely remove these impurities from metal surfaces, but the job should be done by the welder, using a wire brush or an emery cloth. Prior to applying flux, all dirt and grease should be thoroughly removed (Fig. 178).

There are two primary kinds of flux: corrosive and noncorrosive. An example of a corrosize flux is muriatic (hydrochloric) acid, which is best used on hard-to-solder galvanized-iron and sheet-metal surfaces. Rosin, on the other hand, is a commonly used noncorrosive flux, a salt manufactured from crude turpentine. It is used where a tight, corrosive-free joining must be made, such as for electrical connections or for joining copper tubing. New tin is also best soldered with rosin flux, while old tarnished tin may require the use of a corrosive flux, like muriatic acid.

During our high school years, each student enrolled in the metal-shop class was required to make a soldering iron. All forms of soldering were done with this tool, which consisted of a pointed copper head fastened to an iron shaft with a wooden handle. Actually, two soldering irons were made, for two were needed. While one of them was in use, the other was heated by a gasoline-fueled blowtorch. As we remember, it was a lengthy process to "tin" the irons. Their tips were heated to a cherry-red glow, their edges were filed smooth, the solder was applied, and the soldered tip was rubbed on a block of ammonium chloride. After this, other solder would then adhere to the iron. When soldering over one's head, it was necessary to heat and file three of the four edges of the tip to remove the tinning so that molten solder would not drip from the lower edge of the iron into one's face.

The art of soldering has been simplified considerably since World War II. The gasoline blowtorch has been all but replaced with the safer, handier propane torch (Fig. 179), which consists of an inexpensive disposable cartridge filled with liquified petroleum. When propane is released from this cartridge, it converts to a gas that burns readily upon contact with air. A burner assembly with flame tips of various widths can be attached to this propane tank. One tip has a chisel-pointed copper head just like those we made in high school metal shop, although, with the more modern device, both the iron and the torch are an integral tool. A simple valve adjustment controls the amount of gas and, therefore, the amount of heat emitted. Other interchangeable tips include a pencil-flame burner, a blowtorch burner head, and a flame spreader. Being small and lightweight, the propane torch is convenient to use. It heats immediately, requiring no prolonged warm-up period like the gasoline-fueled blowtorch. It operates outdoors in wind; indoors it does not discharge carbon (soot and smoke) or odor.

The electric soldering gun is another post-World War II soldering device (Fig. 180). Its small tip enables it to be used in constricted places. Some will even operate on juice delivered from a 12-volt auto battery, but the most common type sold uses as much as 250 watts of 110-volt electric current. Although these guns often have a double trigger with a low- as well as a high-temperature setting that will operate at 900 degrees Fahrenheit, those quality units generating consistently high temperature while losing heat to the metal being soldered are the most satisfactory to use.

Tools, like the propane canister and the electric soldering gun, now make it possible to perform professional-quality soldering in the homestead workshop. One has only to understand a few basic facts about solder and flux to make possible this level of workmanship.

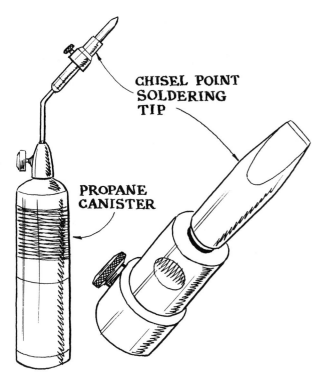

CHISEL POINT SOLDERING TIP

PROPANE CANISTER

Figure 179.

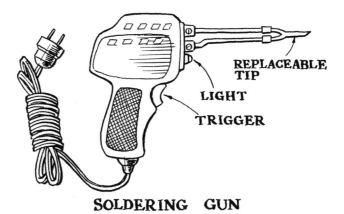

REPLACEABLE TIP

LIGHT

TRIGGER

SOLDERING GUN

Figure 180.

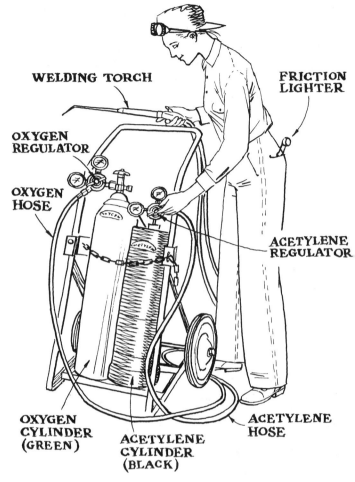

WELDING TORCH

FRICTION LIGHTER

OXYGEN REGULATOR

OXYGEN HOSE

ACETYLENE REGULATOR

OXYGEN CYLINDER (GREEN)

ACETYLENE CYLINDER (BLACK)

ACETYLENE HOSE

Figure 181.

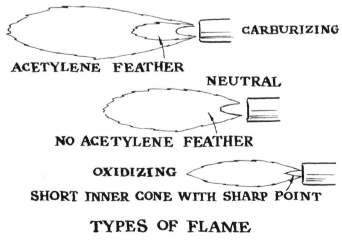

CARBURIZING

ACETYLENE FEATHER

NEUTRAL

NO ACETYLENE FEATHER

OXIDIZING

SHORT INNER CONE WITH SHARP POINT

TYPES OF FLAME

Figure 182.

Chapter 16
GAS WELDING

When a propane soldering torch ignites, its fuel mixes with oxygen in the air, resulting in a flame of intense heat. If we regulate the ratio of propane to oxygen, even greater temperatures can be reached: a one-to-one ratio produces a temperature of 5000 degrees Fahrenheit, while a two-to-one ratio of oxygen to propane will produce a temperature of 6000 degrees Fahrenheit. Gas welding is done with intense heat produced by burning either of two gases—propane or acetylene—in the presence of oxygen. The oxygen itself does not burn but, as a catalyst, it makes elevated temperatures possible.

This generalized explanation illustrates the fact that gas welding requires using pressurized holding tanks and valves to regulate the pressure and flow of gas. Three distinct types of flame are produced by valve adjustment (Fig. 182). If too much oxygen is present, the flame is said to be oxidizing, that is, both the inner white flame as well as the outer flame are short and pointed. Many welders prefer to use an oxidizing flame for brazing metals since its heat is less intense. A second type of flame is indicative of an excess of acetylene and is said to be carburizing. It has a long bluish outer flame, a long inner core, and a yellow middle flare, called an acetylene feather. A carburizing flame should be avoided if a scaly high-carbon weld is not wanted. Rather, a neutral flame should be sought for gas welding. In this flame, the inner core is longer and more blunt and there is no acetylene feather, only a bluish outer flame.

Two distinct steps must be followed in order to obtain a proper welding flame. For the first step, the acetylene valve is opened and the torch is lighted. The opening size of the tip should be predetermined by the thickness of the metal to be welded. The thicker the metal, the larger the opening of the tip. Tip size also determines the necessary gas pressure, which may vary from three pounds for very light metal to twelve pounds for heavier metal. When the tip is lit, the proper pressure setting will produce a slight gap, about ¼ inch, between the tip and the end of the flame. Before the next step is taken, this gap should be adjusted back to a point where the flame just begins to leave the tip; this is the correct acetylene adjustment. For step two, the oxygen valve is slowly opened. First, a yellow flame becomes apparent, one that gradually turns blue as the valve opening is increased. The three distinct oxidizing flame zones also appear: the bright white inner flame, the middle yellow one, and the outer bluish flare. The middle zone will gradually disappear as the oxygen valve is opened more fully and as a neutral flame appears.

We recommend that the beginner shopworker use a flux-coated bronze rod for most gas-fueled welding projects. This type of gas welding is similar to solder welding in that the filler is softer than the base metal, requiring less intense heat to do the job and giving the resulting connection or fastening tremendous strength. A flux coating on the outside of a welding rod serves the same purpose as that in the rod with a solder core, helping the bronze stick to the metal by preventing the formation of oxides. When a bronze rod is used, the welding process is called brazing. Less heat is required to braze than for fusion welding. Therefore, there is less warpage and the brazing of a wider variety of metals is possible. The temperature applied to base metals should never produce a color of flame exceeding that of a salmon red.

In general, the size of the filler rod is equal to the thickness of the base metal, that is, a 3⁄16-inch welding rod is used for joining 3⁄16-inch-thick sheet metal.

Gas welding is only slightly more complicated than solder welding. But once a few elementary motions are learned, one can begin to weld adequately after an hour's practice. First, learn to hold the torch like a hammer. For flat work, always move the torch from right to left. Both rod and torch are held at an angle of 45 degrees to the horizon, but move in opposite directions (as illustrated in Figure 183). Thus the flame preheats the metal in front of the weld, permitting an even flow of weld as the rod is moved along. The tip of the torch should point directly along the weld line, but is held about a quarter inch above the surface. This keeps the flame of the inner core about half the distance from the metal. Because of the intense heat in this inner core, the welding tip must constantly be moved in a semicircular motion; otherwise, the base metal will burn through.

The welding rod also is moved along in a curving motion, puddling between the metal pieces as it moves. If a thin piece of metal is welded to a thicker one, more heat must be directed at the heavier piece.

A "bead" is formed as the puddle of molten bronze is placed in the joint between the pieces of metal being welded. The ability to "lay a bead" is the mark of an experienced welder. To properly do this activity requires good timing. Not only must the circular motion of the torch be coordinated to the temperature of the inner core and the thickness of the metal, but movement of the rod must also be coordinated to these variables and to the speed of movement. If the operation moves too quickly, there will be inadequate melting of rod and metal; if timing is too slow, holes will be melted through the metal. If the rod melts before the base metal receives adequate heat, globules of brass will float on the surface. The end of the welding rod often will stick to a surface that is insufficiently heated. All these difficulties can be remedied with experience (see Figure 184).

The ability to cut metal is an important advantage of having a gas welder in your homestead shop. When metal can be cut easily and efficiently, new avenues of metalworking open up. Innumerable articles can be created in the workshop when thick pieces of scrap metal may be both cut and welded to make new configurations.

A special cutting head must be attached to the torch to cut metal. It has a number of small jets around a larger jet located in the middle of the tip. The peripheral jets emit an oxyacetylene heating flame and the central jet supplies a stream of oxygen under high pressure. Once the metal is sufficiently preheated, the single jet of oxygen does the actual cutting (Fig. 185). Thus higher oxygen pressure—forty pounds rather than eight—is necessary when cutting than is needed when welding, depending on the tip size and the thickness of the metal to be cut. The stream of oxygen is controlled by a lever on the cutting torch. Depressing the lever oxidizes the hot iron, forming iron oxide, which blows off in the form of slag. If there is a high carbon content in the metal, cutting becomes more difficult, for the oxidation process is hindered. The purer the iron, the easier it is to cut. Cutting speed is also determined by the thickness of the metal being cut. A slight forward tilt to the cutting torch should be maintained so that the metal, in advance of the cut, can be heated.

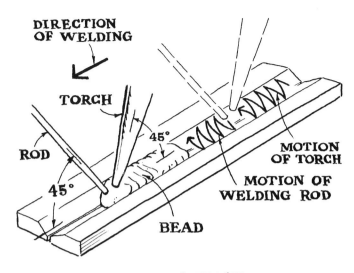

DIRECTION OF WELDING

TORCH

ROD

45°

45°

MOTION OF TORCH

MOTION OF WELDING ROD

BEAD

LAYING A BEAD

Figure 183.

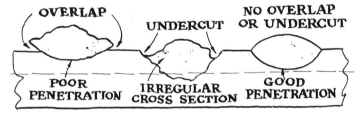

OVERLAP

UNDERCUT

NO OVERLAP OR UNDERCUT

POOR PENETRATION

IRREGULAR CROSS SECTION

GOOD PENETRATION

CROSS SECTIONS OF BEADS

Figure 184.

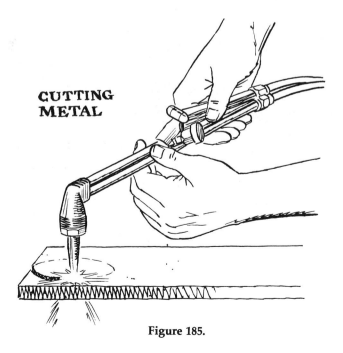

CUTTING METAL

Figure 185.

Figure 186. *Gasoline-powered welder and a. c. generator.*

Chapter 17
ARC WELDING

There is a major leap from solder welding at temperatures below 800 degrees Fahrenheit to arc welding at temperatures above 6000 degrees Fahrenheit. With soldering, a low-temperature filler is melted; but in the case of arc welding, the hard base metal itself is actually fused. The intense heat needed to do this kind of welding results from passing an electric current across a gap of air between the material welded and a steel filler rod. In the fusion process, the filler rod also melts, adding strength to the weld by occupying voids and adding extra material to the joint.

The device producing this intense heat is nothing more than an electric transformer. Regular high voltage (110 or 220) and low amperage (30) are converted to high amperage (up to 700) and low-voltage alternating current (a.c.). Where commercial electric power is not available or is not wanted, as in our particular case, alternating current must be generated with a gasoline-powered generator, pictured in Figure 186. A revolving armature generator of this type—a somewhat more durable unit—will also produce direct current (d.c.). Its main advantage is that, being trailer-mounted, it can be wheeled to most job sites.

Most homestead welding tasks can be performed with a 200-ampere-capacity a.c. transformer welder. The Lincoln Company makes a 180-amp. and a 225-amp. unit, both favored by farmers since the 1920s. Initial cost is low and operation is economical, for there are no moving parts. Furthermore, an arc welder is as easy to use as a soldering iron. In fact, if one had to choose a single tool to do most of the fastening tasks on the homestead, an arc welder could easily be selected. With this one tool, metal of practically any thickness can be permanently fused. Rod, from 1/16-inch diameter to 3/8-inch diameter, can be bought and an equally wide range of temperature settings can be dialed on this machine. Many different metals are welded with specially manufactured filler rods, corresponding to the metal used, such as cast iron, sheet metal, high carbon steel, or stainless steel. When using a carbon-arc attachment (Fig. 187)

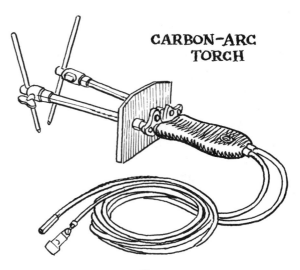

CARBON-ARC TORCH

Figure 187.

on the welder, metal can be cut, heated for bending, brazed, or soldered. Some welders can even be adapted to charge car batteries.

Flux coating the outside of the arc-welding rod has a slightly different function than that coating the brazing rod or that found in the core of the soldering rod. Because higher heat is required for an arc-welded bond, there is a tendency for the base metal to boil. When this molten mass contacts with air, it becomes pock-marked with gas cavities, weakening the bond. But when a thick layer of flux coats the rod, it floats air-laden metal to the surface and also covers it with an insulating layer of flux while the metal cools. A final operation removes this outer layer, called slag. The quality of welding workmanship can be judged by the ease with which slag is finally removed from metal surfaces.

Welding skill is measured by the time that metal remains in a molten state. The longer it remains molten, the less gas escapes and the less slag floats to the surface. The trick, then, is to constantly move the rod in a curving motion, parallel to the line of travel and from one side of the welded surface to the other. This motion is not unlike that used in brazing. Inexperienced welders tend to move the rod too rapidly along the line of travel (see Figure 188) causing an overlap along the edge of the weld where penetration is poor. The opposite may occur when movement is too slow; when this happens, edges of the metal are undercut and penetration is excessive. A good rule of thumb to follow is that the length of bead should equal the length of rod used. The weld will penetrate half the thickness of the rod for a width twice the thickness of the rod. The thicker the base metal, the thicker the rod must be in order to carry the higher amperage necessary to fuse the metal.

Another important arc-welding technique requires accurate spacing between the rod and the molten metal; that is, its arc length (Fig. 189). Too high an arc will produce a wide, flat bead with much spattering; too short an arc will produce a narrow, high bead that is porous and weak. The proper length depends on many factors—the amount of heat used, the type and thickness of the rod, the type of metal being welded, etc. But as a general rule, arc distance should be equal to the thickness of the rod.

Start the weld by first touching the rod to the material with a sweeping motion, much like striking a match. This causes the current to flow. The rod is then immediately held at proper arc length, leaning the top about 20 degrees in the direction of the welding (Fig. 190). It is then slowly and steadily moved from left to right across the material as the rod is woven back and forth into the metal.

Welding rods are color coded, number coded, and available in many thicknesses. Flux coloring can be used as an indicator for correct temperature setting. Once a rod is spent, if the color of the remaining stub has changed appreciably, the amperage was set too high and should be lowered before continuing the weld. The first three numbers are indicators of what the rod will do. For example, we use No. 6011 rod for general purpose welding. The first two digits, *60*, indicate that the rod is adequate to support 60,000 pounds of tensile strength per square inch. If greater strength is required, use a No. 7011 rod. The third digit, *1*, refers to the welding position in which the rod may be held. A *1* means any position, a *2* means downhand and horizontal positions, and a *3* means downhand position only (Fig. 191). A downhand position is one in which welding is done from the upper side of a joint. The face of the weld is flat; it uses gravity to advantage, for large amounts of filler can be deposited rapidly as compared with overhead or vertical welding.

At the center of our welding work space, we have built a 36-inch-high table (B3) of 28-inch x 32-inch steel plate (Fig. 193, position△). It is mounted on a single 4-inch pipe pedestal buried in a 2-foot-thick block of concrete. This welding table is handy for any type of heavy-duty hammering, for it functions as a substitute anvil as well. Above the table on panel W5, we have mounted all tools associated with the oxyacetylene or arc welder:

- brazing rod
- arc-welding rod
- oil can
- handled wire brush
- chipping hammer
- head shield for arc welding with lift-up lens
- C clamps (two each: 6 inch and 8 inch) (see Fig. 192); locking C clamps (two each: 3 inch and 10 inch)
- clear goggles
- welding goggles
- one set tip cleaners
- gas welding tips: sizes 1, 2, 3, 5, 7 (Smith sizes)
- cutting attachment
- cutting tips: sizes 2, 4, 6 (Smith sizes)
- friction flint lighter

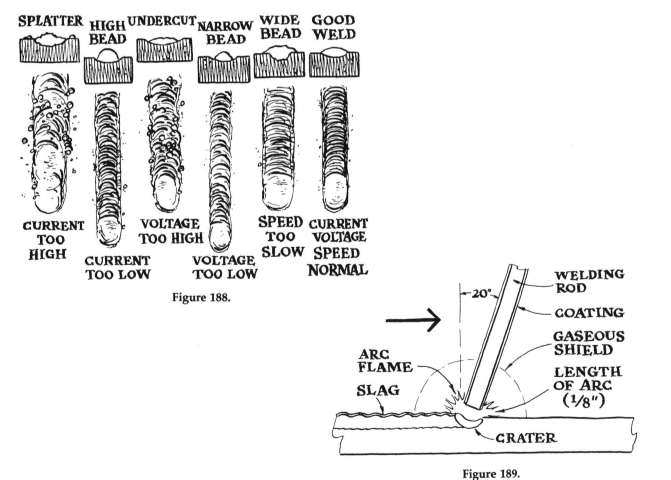

SPLATTER **HIGH BEAD** **UNDERCUT** **NARROW BEAD** **WIDE BEAD** **GOOD WELD**

CURRENT TOO HIGH **CURRENT TOO LOW** **VOLTAGE TOO HIGH** **VOLTAGE TOO LOW** **SPEED TOO SLOW** **CURRENT VOLTAGE SPEED NORMAL**

Figure 188.

WELDING ROD
COATING
GASEOUS SHIELD
LENGTH OF ARC (1/8")
20°
ARC FLAME
SLAG
CRATER

Figure 189.

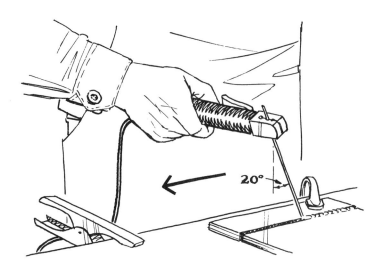

ARC WELDING

Figure 190.

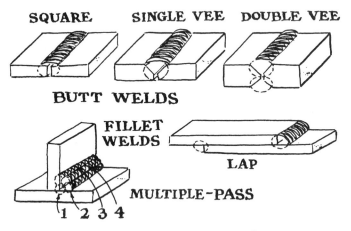

SQUARE   SINGLE VEE   DOUBLE VEE

BUTT WELDS

FILLET WELDS

LAP

MULTIPLE-PASS

1 2 3 4

WELDING JOINTS

Figure 191.

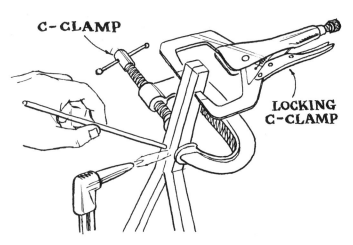

C-CLAMP

LOCKING C-CLAMP

Figure 192.

Figure 193. *In the center of the welding work space is a 36-inch-high table of steel plate and above the table are mounted all tools associated with the oxyacetylene or arc welder.* Photo by Michael Eckerman

Figure 194. *The "grease pit" for underchassis work.* Photo by Michael Eckerman

Chapter 18
THE POLITICS OF MOTOR VEHICLE USE

The area of the workshop in which we maintain and repair our motor vehicles is a fundamental and vital part of the homestead. At the north end of our shop is a storage cabinet for spare engine parts and the grease pit for under-chassis work, over which there is a rail-mounted hoist for removing an engine from a vehicle (Fig. 194, position △). Automotive tools (discussed in the next chapter) are kept in chests nearby beneath the metalworking bench (BS2).

To maintain an operating vehicle on the homeplace is, at best, a compromise. Autos or trucks become major impediments to homesteading self-sufficiency when they require as much as a third of a family's disposable income to purchase, operate, and maintain them.

The automobile industry and closely associated petroleum companies together wield an overpowering influence on the economy of the world, on increased pollution of our environment, on the use of nonrenewable energy resources, on the urbanization of our countryside, on people's employment opportunities and personal safety, and on our government's policies with foreign countries. These two huge industries are responsible for half of our Gross National Product. If the annual budgets of Exxon and General Motors were combined, it would be the third highest in the world, surpassed only by two *nations*—the United States and the Soviet Union.

With such power and capital centralized in a few companies, one might expect exceptional products from them. But no . . . if this were actually the case, our own homestead-shop design would be different; the vehicle repair and maintenance wing would not command such prominence and space. The extent of this facility is necessary only because motor vehicles are excessively faulty, both in their design and in their manufacture. To understand our approach to automotive repair and maintenance, we wish to share the following views to introduce this part of our shop.

Products of the auto industry are exceptional—exceptionally faulty. In a recent study for the U.S. Department of Transportation done by the Auto Club of America, 8000 cars were examined and three-fourths were found to have at least one potentially dangerous defect. These were vehicles considered safe enough to be exempted from company recall. One out of two cars manufactured between 1966 and 1973 were recalled—40 million of them. This figure includes 10,000 school buses that General Motors recalled for defective brakes. Admittedly, faulty auto design and manufacture are only partly responsible for the 55,000 deaths and the 3 million injuries from auto accidents each year. More people have, however, been killed in fifty years' use of the automobile than from all wars fought in the two-hundred-year history of this nation. The automobile is the largest cause of death for people between the ages of fifteen and thirty-four.

Then, there are the uncounted living victims

of automobile use. Emphysema, the fastest growing killer disease in this country, is directly attributed to air pollution, to which the ubiquitous internal-combustion engine daily contributes hundreds of tons of unburned hazardous products. Most carbon monoxide emissions are also a product of this engine. With high affinity for oxygen, carbon monoxide contributes its part to the eventual asphyxiation of the human race. These two pollutants also contribute to the rapid increase in heart and vascular disease, bronchitis, stroke, and lung cancer. In heavily polluted areas, like Los Angeles, the mortality rate for these diseases is phenomenally higher than for rural areas. Air pollution also results from lead emissions from gasoline, causing anemia and damage to the central nervous system. Unburned hydrocarbons are in part responsible for the rise in lung cancer, while asbestos fibers spewed into the air from auto brake linings contribute to heart and lung disease as well.

We do not anticipate that much improvement in the environment will come from regulatory agencies of the federal government or from the auto and oil industries themselves. Smog-control devices now in use cause more fuel to be burned and engine parts to wear out faster because engines run hotter than those in automobiles without such devices. The only way we can breathe cleaner air is to abandon the internal-combustion engine. This, however, is not likely since auto manufacturers have little incentive to retool to make a new engine when current designs still provide them with bloated profits. Too, the ultimate decision is not so much in the hands of engine producers as it is with the all-powerful oil companies. As long as enormous profits are made by supplying petroleum products to operate the internal-combustion engine, this design will remain a part of our existence.

While consumer safety and environmental pollution are two of the biggest issues involved in general motor-vehicle use today, factors that influence our automotive work are those involving car or truck design and assembly. Again, the facts are equally depressing. For the most part, automobiles are poorly assembled at the factory: engines are not designed for easy accessibility of repair; vehicles seem purposely designed to be easily damaged; and parts lack standardization and are intended to be replaced, not repaired, providing manufacturers with more profit from additional sales. According to the Consumers Union, a third of the $30 billion spent yearly on auto repair is for work that need not have been done. Many studies and even a few Congressional hearings have reviewed the bilking of the American motorist by operators of automotive repair shops. Too often, however, even the auto mechanic is a victim of producers' products, which are poorly made, difficult to work on, and inordinately expensive.

Automotive repair costs are usually figured from a flat-rate manual rather than by actual hours worked. Thus, changing the spark plugs on a certain late-model Ford costs the hapless car owner a mechanic's labor charge of $80. The reason? To perform this simple necessary chore, the engine must be partially removed from the chassis. Even to replace a turn-signal bulb on a late-model Cadillac the car's bumper must first be removed. The charge for labor to change a $1 light bulb is $20.

Twenty years ago when we built our first homestead workshop, we surveyed our family's transportation needs and decided, *Number One*, never to pay more than $200 for any vehicle. With inflation, this cost would now more likely be $500, although one can still find numerous older running vehicles for $200. The functional life of automobiles becomes less with each passing year; the average life of a car is now ten years whereas it was fifteen years twenty years ago. For those entrenched in the money economy, it is easier to replace an auto than to repair it. In one recent year, 8 million cars were junked while 12 million were built to replace them.

On a homestead, where there is more time than money, it is best to buy a junked vehicle for rebuilding as a homestead conveyance. In other words, *Number Two*, do all the work yourself. This, of course, can only be done after you have built a workshop and learned the necessary skills for automotive repair, refurbishing, and maintenance. In the following chapter, we briefly describe what is required to do this kind of work. Essentially, all internal-combustion engines are designed to work in the same manner. Basic automotive engineering was developed prior to World War II, the self-starter being the last major improvement made. Newer engines are now built with closer tolerances so they can go faster, making them more difficult to work on. This brings us to principle *Number Three:* standardize on the vehicle make and model you will use, one that is American-made and/or commonly available so that securing inexpensive parts should never be a problem. Your choice should be the best-built vehicle to come out of Detroit (or elsewhere) so that its parts will last longer. It should be easy to work on without your having to buy or use specialized tools. In our opinion, the most practical all-around useful homestead vehicle is the half-ton pickup truck.

Twenty years ago we also decided that our automotive standard bearer would be a 1954 model 270 6-cylinder GMC ¾-ton flatbed truck. We have run such a vehicle ever since. In time, we have accumulated a number of these vintage pickups, mostly for spare parts. There are 2500 major parts in a motor vehicle. Counting every nut and bolt, the number of individual parts amounts to about 20,000 per vehicle. If all were bought separately, their money value would be considerable. A few years ago someone priced the retail cost for all parts for a new Chevrolet selling for $3500. The total came to $7500, and the cost of labor to assemble them, in order to build a running vehicle, was another $7500.

Our solution was, therefore, to standardize vehicles, using one make and model of auto and, whenever possible, purchasing junked vehicles of the same model for spare parts. Operating expenditures for our vehicle over a twenty-year period have averaged $200 yearly, providing us with dependable truck transportation. It is important for the homesteader, however, to maintain precisely the same year and model, for manufacturers often make mid-year parts changes with little reason other than to prevent parts standardization. In 1948, Henry Ford found that only two muffler/tail-pipe assemblies were needed for all models his company built. Twenty years later, Ford automobiles used no fewer than fifty-six different muffler/tail-pipe designs.

It is difficult for us to fathom how people permit themselves to be hyped into new-car purchase, although it is a temptation to which most Americans, ourselves included, have at one time or another succumbed. Fully a third of one's new-car investment is immediately (within the first year) usurped by annual style changes. Another devaluation is your new car's planned obsolescence backed by worthless warranties. We forget that the trap of consumer credit was originally sparked by the auto industry, principally by General Motors. We also forget that plastic money, the credit card, was first manufactured and distributed by oil companies. The perceptive homesteader may, at least, try to reverse this trend, and we attempt in the following chapter to explain how this may be done.

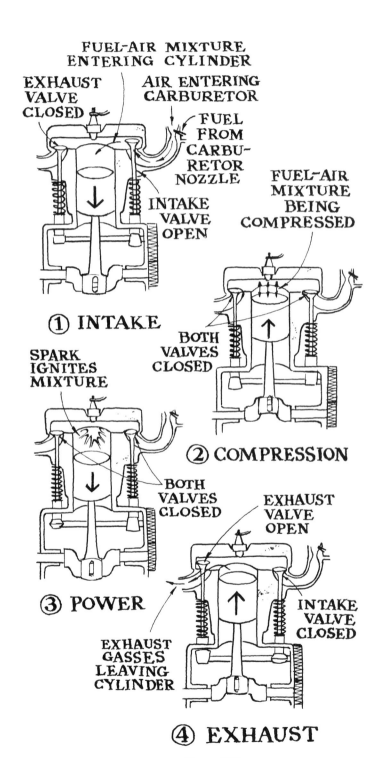

FUEL-AIR MIXTURE
ENTERING CYLINDER

EXHAUST
VALVE
CLOSED

AIR ENTERING
CARBURETOR

FUEL
FROM
CARBU-
RETOR
NOZZLE

INTAKE
VALVE
OPEN

FUEL-AIR
MIXTURE
BEING
COMPRESSED

① INTAKE

BOTH
VALVES
CLOSED

② COMPRESSION

SPARK
IGNITES
MIXTURE

BOTH
VALVES
CLOSED

EXHAUST
VALVE
OPEN

③ POWER

INTAKE
VALVE
CLOSED

EXHAUST
GASSES
LEAVING
CYLINDER

④ EXHAUST

Figure 195.

Chapter 19
THE ENGINE SYSTEM

The best way to understand a complicated system, like an automobile engine, is to break it down into its interdependent parts. In a motor vehicle, the *engine* (a machine using energy to develop mechanical power) uses *fuel* (burnable material) to power a drive train which turns its wheels. The engine is *started* (set in operation) when ignition (spark) is applied to the fuel in its combustion (firing) chambers. When performing, the engine must *charge* the battery (replenish its stored electrical charge) and *cool* itself (reduce its temperature). *Exhaust* gases (or spent fuel) must be removed. The whole assembly is *suspended* (supported on springs) on its undercarriage or axles and may be *steered* and *braked* at will. Thus a dozen different reciprocal systems are indispensable to the operation of a motor vehicle. Each must be discussed relative to its propensity for maintenance and repair in our homestead workshop.

The term "internal combustion" describes that kind of engine in common use in virtually all motor vehicles today. *In* its cylinders, fuel is burned to produce the power or force to push pistons which activate a drive line. A steam engine, on the other hand, is fired by what is called "external combustion," because pistons or plungers in its cylinders are fired or moved by a source of *external* heat, generally steam from a boiler. Either of these engines produces heat (energy) by combustion (burning) and converts it to mechanical energy to produce motion. In the cylinder chamber, a gaseous fuel

mixture is compressed (or squeezed) by the upstroke of a piston, increasing its temperature. In this state, the fuel mixture is readily ignited by an electrical spark delivered from the vehicle's electrical system. The ensuing explosion forces the head of the piston downward. Its vertical up-and-down motion must next be converted to the horizontal turning motion of the drive line. This is accomplished simply by attaching the piston head to a rod (or metal shaft). The lower looped end of the rod revolves at a right angle about the crank (that part of an offset crankshaft which transmits motion). For engine response to occur, three things are essential: a fuel supply, air to supply oxygen for fuel combustion, and ignition to spark an explosion of the air-gas mixture.

Automobile engines are designated as "four-cycle" machines because one complete downward/upward period of piston movement is composed of four stages, or strokes as they are called (Fig. 195). The *intake* stroke is first, during which the piston starts its downward movement in the cylinder chamber. As this happens, a vacuum is created in the top of the cylinder, above the downward-moving piston. An air-gas fuel mixture is drawn or sucked into this part of the chamber to fill this vacuum. At the end of the intake stroke, the crank turns, pushing the rod and piston upward. This motion compacts gaseous fuel received from the mixing chamber, called the carburetor, in the upper part of the cylinder and is called the *compression* stroke. As compressed hot gases ignite from an electrical spark delivered from a plug carrying an electrical current from the storage battery to the cylinder, the *power* stroke forces the piston downward once again. With completion of the power stroke, burned gases are flushed from the chamber with an *exhaust* stroke. The opening and closing of valves defines these distinct strokes. There is one set of valves for the intake of fuel and another to exhaust spent fuel. The opening and closing of valves and the ignition spark must be timed to fire correctly for smooth engine performance. This is accomplished by the camshaft, which is connected to and carefully synchronized by gears with the crankshaft. Note, too, that both valve inlets and valve outlets open directly into the cylinder—one admits fuel mixture and one discharges burned gases. As more cylinders are added to an engine to increase its power, the timing of valve and ignition functions becomes crucial. All exhaust gases must depart the cylinder before intake valves open. This function can be fine tuned by adjusting the firing of the ignition so that spark occurs slightly in advance of the highest point of the piston's compressive stroke. Therefore, ignition occurs slightly before the downward power stroke and must be coordinated with the movement of the piston.

Lubrication is essential to proper engine functioning. To lubricate means to make smooth or slippery, and in an engine it is oil that prevents the metal-to-metal contact of engine parts which would otherwise cause friction and power loss. Oil also cleans and removes heat from engine parts. A film of oil provides a final seal between piston rings and cylinder walls. Oil is pumped through a filter into numerous engine passageways to coat various bearings and gears. It then flows back to the crankcase or pan, a large-capacity container located below the engine, where it is cooled by air rushing beneath the moving vehicle.

Crankcase oil gets dirty but does not wear out. Years ago, we installed one of the first Frantz oil-filter holders in our lubricating system. We have replaced the inexpensive toilet-paper filter used in this holder every thousand miles. By adding a quart of oil each time the soiled filter was removed, we maintained a cleaner engine than if we had regularly resorted to the usual 5000-mile oil change and filter replacement. The oil in one of our GMC pickups was not changed in eight years of regular use. When we disassembled its engine to replace piston rings and grind valves, we found no sludge in the crankcase and all crankshaft bearings were in excellent condition despite 80,000 miles of wear. The engine had begun to burn a quart of oil every 200 miles, an indication that piston rings or valve guides were worn or that crankshaft bearings needed replacement.

The most accurate diagnostic test for an engine that has begun to burn more oil than normal is done with a compression gauge. This tool reveals whether some of the compressed gas-air mixture in the cylinder is escaping past worn piston rings into the cylinder chamber proper. A compression test is easily done: just remove all spark plugs and, while the engine is cranked over a few times by turning the ignition key to advance the spark and activate the starter motor, insert the compression tester in each spark-plug hole. The cylinder fires and a pressure reading from the compression-tester dial is taken for each cylinder. Repeat this process a second time, but before taking a reading, squirt a teaspoon of oil into each cylinder (through the spark-plug hole). The oil will seal the rings, increasing compression so that the second compression reading will be 10–20 pounds more than the first. If an increase or spread of 30 pounds or more is registered, piston rings or cylinder walls are likely to be worn. If most cylinder readings are about equal but one varies by 20 or more pounds, a problem is indicated in that cylinder.

A compression test also indicates the condition of engine valves; a reading of zero indicates, for instance, that a valve is badly burned. A vacuum reading, however, will reveal more about the condition of valves than a compression reading. As mentioned previously, a vacuum is created in a cylinder as the piston moves downward during the intake stroke. At this time, the intake valve opens and fuel is drawn from the carburetor into the intake manifold and then into the combustion chamber. There should be a steady, constant vacuum as each cylinder draws fuel. Depending upon the movement of the vacuum-gauge needle, a malfunction is shown as due either to a sticking valve, an improperly adjusted carburetor, a leaky head gasket, or another possible problem. A constant vacuum reading of from 17 to 22 inches of pressure for an idling engine is considered acceptable. When the throttle is rapidly opened and closed on a properly tuned engine, the vacuum needle should drop toward 0 and jump back beyond a reading of 20.

Much information about the interior condition of an engine may be determined by inspecting its spark plugs. In a properly working engine, a spark-plug electrode (its metal tip) should be tan or light brown in color. Depending on the kind of deposit laid down on this electrode, an engine is shown to be running too hot, too rich, or too lean, or to be fouled with oil or water. Often, the condition of spark plugs will indicate mistiming; that is, the ignition spark is not delivered to the cylinder at precisely the right moment. A timing light is an indispensable tool with which to adjust the timing (or firing) of the ignition spark. With the engine idling, the timing light is attached to the spark plug on the cylinder. It displays a flash of light at each instant the cylinder fires. This light is aimed at the spinning pulley in front of the engine. This pulley has a notch that should line up with a metal pointer/indicator welded to the engine block in this area. The timing light should flash at the very moment the notch on the pulley and the pointer on the engine block align. If they do not, the engine's firing is out of time or synchronization. To correct this, merely loosen the distributor anchor bolt and twist the body of the distributor back and forth until the timing light shows true adjustment. While you have your hand on the distributor, remove its cap and inspect its rotor, points, and condenser. Points open and close, making contact about 10,000 times each minute. It is a simple matter to replace ignition parts, some-

thing that should be done every 5000 miles.

This type of engine work falls into the category of maintenance and tune-up, the most elemental activity of vehicle care the owner-driver will perform. Automobile manufacturers, however, do not encourage backyard mechanics. Some consumer groups complain that car manufacturers issue classified service bulletins that are available only to the service departments of franchised auto dealers. The owner's manual tucked in the glove compartment of every new automobile tells little more than how to operate the cigarette lighter or empty the ashtray. For that matter, nationwide surveys from automobile dealers report that only about 3 percent of new-car buyers even bother to look under the hood.

It is essential to consult a bona fide repair manual specifically written for your engine before you attempt engine maintenance, tune-up, or repair. These books are often not available, as they should be, from the vehicle dealer or manufacturer. But they may be purchased from private publishers, like Motors (1790 Broadway, N.Y., NY 10019) or Chilton (Radnor, PA 19089). Both companies have repair manuals for vehicles produced as far back as 1940.

Consulting a clearly written repair manual, using a few essential tools, having a well-ordered shop in which to work, and plenty of unhurried time, you can learn to completely rebuild the engine of your homestead vehicle. This operation includes replacing piston rings and rod bearings, installing a new crankshaft kit (which includes regrinding the crankshaft and replacing bearings, usually done by a professional), seating new valves, and generally cleaning parts and replacing gaskets. Virtually any replacement part is available from discount auto stores or from mail-order catalogs, like J. C. Whitney & Co. (1917-19 Archer St., Box 8410, Chicago, IL 60680). This company also sells a complete line of Motors or Chilton repair manuals and all necessary tools.

An investment in tools can be recovered with the first engine overhaul. A ridge reamer is necessary to remove the lip that results from piston-ring wear on cylinder walls. This ridge must be removed before pistons may be removed and replaced. A cylinder-wall hone scours cylinder walls to break the glaze that forms as a result of piston-ring wear. A piston-groove cleaner cuts the carbon buildup in the grooves on piston heads prior to new ring replacement. A piston-ring expander will remove or install used piston rings without breakage. A piston-ring compressor will install new rings in an engine block. A valve lifter removes valves from the engine head. A valve grinder properly seats resurfaced valves. A torque wrench is used to replace head bolts. Equal and exact tightening of bolts prevents warpage, cracking, and leaking gaskets.

This brief introduction to engine operation, maintenance, and repair is intended only to encourage homestead shop mechanics to involve themselves in all facets of engine care, from simple lubrication to engine rebuilding. We derive much satisfaction from assuming responsibility for the care and repair of our homestead vehicles.

Figure 196. *Engine repair tools: container, torque wrench, groove cleaner, valve lifter, ring compressor, valve grinder, compression gauge, vacuum gauge, timing light, brake-cylinder hone, ridge reamer, micrometers, cylinder-wall hone, and piston-groove cleaner.*

Figure 197. *Engine repair tools on multipurpose movable bench.*

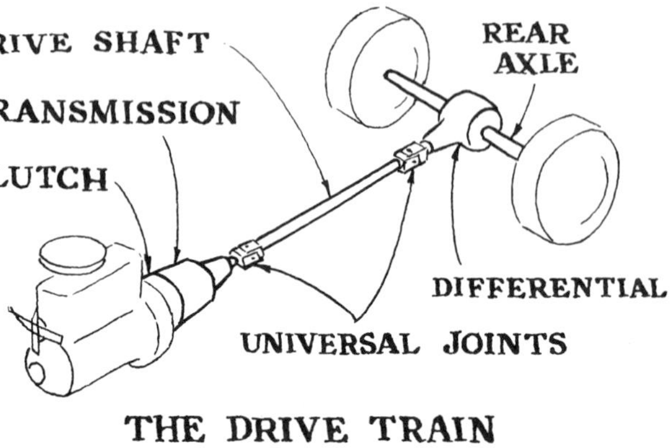

DRIVE SHAFT

TRANSMISSION

CLUTCH

REAR
AXLE

DIFFERENTIAL

UNIVERSAL JOINTS

THE DRIVE TRAIN

Figure 198.

Chapter 20
AUTOMOTIVE SYSTEMS

In the previous chapter, it was noted that there are a dozen interdependent systems in the motor vehicle that must be maintained and kept in repair. Of these, we detailed the most prominent, the engine. Here we will touch on the other eleven components, suggesting how a homestead mechanic may best maintain each of them and what special kinds of tools are required to do this work.

THE DRIVE TRAIN

The drive train of a motor vehicle is a series of connected mechanical parts that delivers motion, generated by the engine, to the vehicle's wheels, causing them to turn (Fig. 198). The first of these parts, the clutch, is an intermediary apparatus, by means of which gears on the crankshaft are temporarily connected to or disengaged from gears on the drive train. For vehicles in which gears are manually changed or shifted, the clutch consists of an asbestos-lined plate that contacts a metal plate attached to the turning crankshaft. When the driver engages the clutch pedal, a throwout bearing presses against a series of springs, which release the clutch disc. On occasion, this bearing and the clutch disc must be replaced but no specialized tools are required for this task. (For vehicles in which gears are shifted automatically, the clutch consists of hydraulic cylinders operated by the movement and force of a liquid. The clutch in such a system is not a separate component but is incorporated in the transmission.)

Located directly behind the clutch is the transmission, a device that conveys or transmits force (movement) from the engine to the rear wheels of a vehicle. Variations in the speed of a vehicle are achieved by several gears: high, low, reverse, or neutral. The only upkeep on a transmission is the need to maintain fluid level in the transmission box. The heavy gear oil used to lubricate this system preserves its numerous gears by cooling them.

Next, a metal drive shaft connects the transmission with the driving mechanism in the rear axle. A pair of hingelike universal joints are found on either end of this shaft or line. They permit rotary motion from the drive shaft to be transmitted to the axle shaft, which is at right angles to it. These joints should be greased occasionally, for they receive a great deal of wear.

Vehicles would be unable to turn corners smoothly if it were not for the differential gears, an arrangement of gears connecting the two rear axles in the same line. They divide the driving force between them while allowing one axle to turn faster than the other and permitting a difference in axle speeds while turning curves. Like the transmission, the differential housing should be checked regularly for oil level. Do not attempt to recondition any drive-train components. When these parts break, try to have spare ones on hand to replace those broken.

STEERING

The steering wheel of a vehicle is connected to a long metal column that terminates at a gear box (Fig. 199). A so-called Pitman arm, anchored to this gear box, pushes tie-rods back and forth as the steering wheel is turned in one direction or another. Most of the arms, levers, pins, rods, and joints composing this system have grease fittings that should be attended to regularly. Kingpins connect the wheel assembly to the tie-rods and allow the wheels to swivel or turn from side to side. Rarely are they replaced.

BRAKES

The motion of the vehicle is slowed or stopped by friction resulting from interaction between brake shoes or pads and brake drums or discs (see Figure 200). A hydraulic braking system consists of a master cylinder and four individual wheel cylinders, connected by lines and hoses filled with a special oil that transmits the force of the foot pedal to brake shoes. A customary "brake job" involves exchanging or relining brake shoes, resurfacing brake drums, rebuilding cylinders, and replacing weakened hoses. The fluid level of this system must be maintained, and adjustments must occasionally be made between the shoe and the drum.

FUEL

Gasoline travels from the vehicle's storage tank through a fuel line to a pump that forces it through a cleansing filter into the carburetor (Fig. 201). Air, which must also be clean, passes through an air filter on its way to the carburetor. Here, fuel mixes with air to form a burnable vapor. Then this vaporous mix enters the combustion chamber or cylinder through the intake manifold. Each of these filters should be regularly cleaned or replaced; otherwise, little maintenance is required for the fuel system.

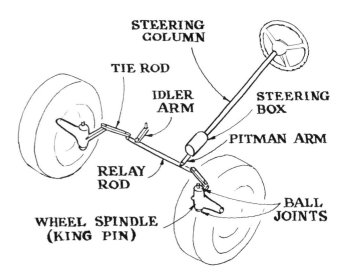

STEERING   Figure 199.

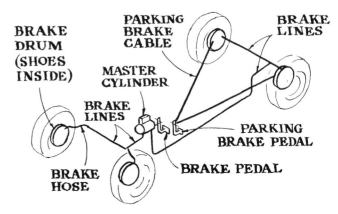

BRAKE SYSTEM   Figure 200.

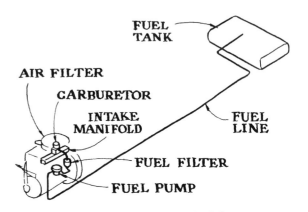

FUEL SYSTEM   Figure 201.

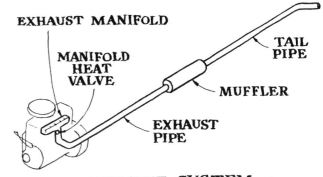

EXHAUST SYSTEM   Figure 202.

EXHAUST

Two things take place in an exhaust system (Fig. 202). First, at the end of each working stroke of the pistons, burned gases are emptied from cylinders through the exhaust manifold and into an exhaust pipe, from which they are discharged into the atmosphere. Second, the noise of combustion explosions is suppressed by a baffle or silencing device on the exhaust pipe, called a muffler. The muffler and exhaust pipe both receive a great amount of heat and frequently may rust out. It is a simple matter to replace the entire system, especially when the homestead has a workshop equipped with a grease pit in which to work beneath a vehicle.

STARTING

To start or turn over an engine, a starting motor is needed to crank the engine into action (Fig. 203). This motor draws its power from a battery through cables connected to a starter switch. When the ignition key is turned on, electrical contact is made to a solenoid switch which relays power from the battery directly to the starter engine. Thus huge amounts of electricity need not be routed through the ignition switch itself. Battery cables, connectors, and the storage battery require frequent attention. Fluid level in the battery should be maintained so that the output of current remains high.

IGNITION

A battery supplies the electrical energy needed to generate a spark, which in turn causes the fuel-air mixture in each cylinder to ignite (Fig. 204). In order to supply the necessary 20,000 volts that cause a spark to jump between the electrodes of a spark plug, current from a 12-volt battery is transformed to a higher voltage by an ignition coil. High-voltage current then passes from the coil to the distributor, which delivers an electric charge to each spark

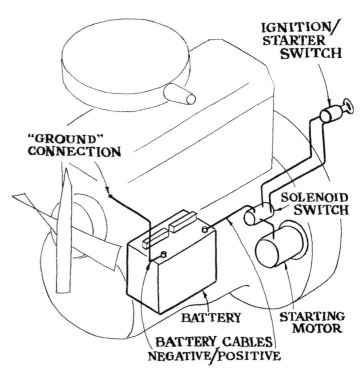

STARTING SYSTEM Figure 203.

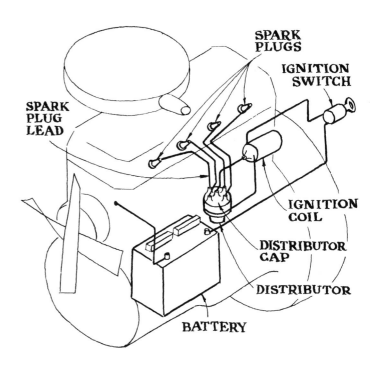

IGNITION SYSTEM Figure 204.

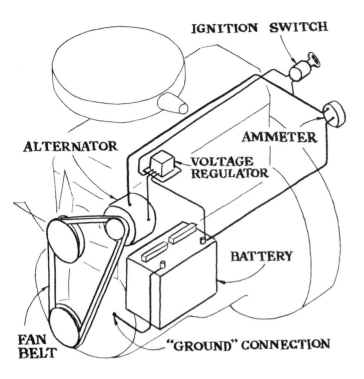

GENERATING SYSTEM

Figure 205.

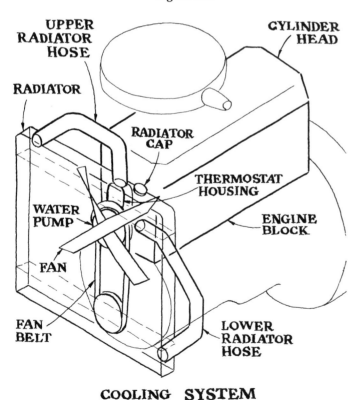

COOLING SYSTEM

Figure 206.

plug independently. This relay is achieved by distributor points that make contact according to the firing order of engine pistons. Spark-plug wires, connectors, the distributor and its parts (points, rotor, condenser), and the distributor cap should all be inspected regularly.

GENERATING

As an engine runs, electrical energy is produced by a generator (or in newer cars by an alternator), Fig. 205. This device is driven by a fan belt located in front of the engine. It is important that this belt be checked periodically for any cuts and for proper tautness. When a surplus of electricity is generated, a relay is sent to the voltage regulator, which prevents extra power from reaching the battery. Conversely, when the battery is low, the voltage regulator allows excess power to flow into it for storage.

COOLING

To keep an engine running cool, the heat of combustion must be conducted away from the cylinders. Generally, water circulates around the engine block and through the small tubes of a radiator, a water-filled apparatus designed to radiate superfluous heat. Circulation is assisted by a water pump and cooling is promoted by a fan blowing cool air between small tubes of the radiator (Fig. 206). Cooled water from the radiator recirculates through the engine, where it picks up more heat and is again pumped through the radiator for cooling. When the engine-radiator water is cold, a thermostat automatically closes off any flow between the engine block and the radiator. As it heats up, however, the thermostat opens to allow hot water access to the radiator. The radiator cap is also a kind of thermostat. When pressure builds up in the system, this cap allows steam to escape, preferably into an overflow reservoir. When the engine cools, water in the reservoir siphons back into the system. Radiator hoses that connect the radiator with the engine block should be inspected periodically. The water pump requires regular greasing.

ELECTRICAL SYSTEM

Electrical wires lead from the battery to headlights and other electrical equipment on the vehicle, such as turn signals, windshield wipers, radio, heater, etc. These various electrical circuits are protected from overloading by a bank of fuses that are easily replaced. A small tin of spare fuses should be kept in the glove compartment.

SUSPENSION

There are two systems of suspension, one in front of the vehicle and one in the rear (Fig. 207). They consist of springs, shock absorbers, and ball-joint stabilizers to keep the frame of the vehicle elevated above its wheels. Suspension also cushions the ride for passengers. All of these parts receive considerable wear and must be lubricated frequently. Occasionally, shock absorbers must be replaced.

When Detroit replaced dashboard gauges with warning or "idiot" lights, they created one of the biggest farces for drivers since publication of the owner's manual. Fortunately, it is possible to replace these "too late" lights with more practical gauges at little cost. Serious motorists must know at all times exactly how well their engine is performing, not just how fast their vehicle is moving or how much fuel remains in the tank. A kit of four gauges with illuminated dials can be purchased from J. C. Whitney's for about $20. They take the guesswork out of engine performance. The engine-temperature range may be read from 100 to 200 degrees Fahrenheit. Amperage readings are seen from a charge of 60 amperes to a discharge of 60 amperes. Oil pressure is shown from 0 to 80 pounds. Vacuum pressure reads from 0 to 30 inches. The vacuum-pressure gauge, known as a "motor monitor," shows at a glance how much fuel is being consumed, for the pressure in an engine intake manifold is directly related to the amount of fuel burned; that is, the higher the vacuum-pressure reading, the more miles traveled for each gallon of fuel burned.

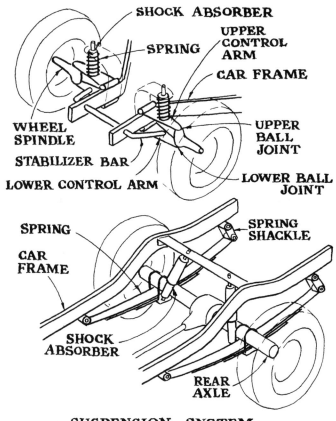

SUSPENSION SYSTEM

Figure 207.

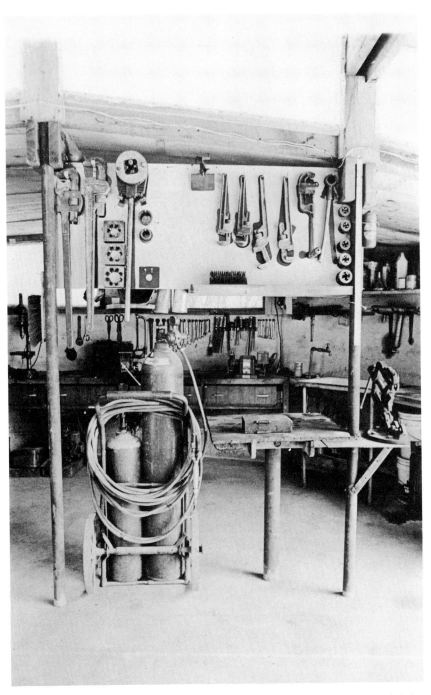

Figure 208. *On the project side of the welding center are tools used to work metal piping.*
Photo by Michael Eckerman

Chapter 21
THE PROJECT AREA

To one side of the welding center (Fig. 208, position⚠) we place those tools used to work metal piping. The heavy iron welding table (B3), which can be worked from three of its sides, replaces the traditional anvil. A 5-inch hinged-jaw vise occupies a place on one corner of this table. Then, by opening the front or rear doors of the shop, full lengths of iron pipe may be accommodated in the space that results. It is important that table and vise be securely anchored, for both, at times, are subject to severe stress when pipe is either tightened or loosened in the grip of vise jaws. Here, the columnar pipe support for the roof beam overhead helps to stabilize both bench and vise. On the panel above the table (W6) is hung the usual assortment of pipe-working tools:

- three sets of pipe wrenches, 36″, 14″, 8″
- pipe cutters, ¼″–2″
- ratchet threaders for small pipe, ⅛″, ¼″, ½″, ¾″
- ratchet threaders for large pipe, 1″, 1¼″, 1½″, 2″
- burr reamers, ¼″–1¼″.

On a small shelf attached at the bottom of the wall panel, cutting oil, pipe compound, and a wire brush are found. A hand broom hangs from the bottom edge of this panel, convenient also to the welding side of the table, for shop use is facilitated by frequent sweeping of work surfaces. Although rags are generally stored in the paint section of the shop, several are kept handy on all work benches, for having them readily available encourages their frequent use. For example, when working with metal, a worker is constantly wiping oil, solvent, water, or rust from work surfaces.

The only item located in the space designated for large projects is our often-used multipurpose portable utility table (Fig. 196). Otherwise, the area is unoccupied and swept clean. A large push broom and scoop shovel hang handy nearby, among a number of yard implements at W7 (Fig. 209, position⚠). Included in this tool selection are a rake, mattock, pickaxe, posthole digger, bolt cutter, high-lift jack, shovel, and sledgehammer.

On the opposite wall (W8), we store yard implements (Fig. 210, position⚠) used to harvest the homestead's firewood and to build and repair fencing. On the end of this panel, across from the wood heater, hang a wood-splitting hatchet and fence pliers. Suspended from the panel's face are an adze, splitting maul, double-bitted axe, brush axe, machete, splitting axe, pry bar, come-along, fence stretcher, post driver, and a crosscut timber saw. Suspended by hook and chain from the roof beam above the panel is a gas-powered brush-and-weed cutter.

The hatchet hanging at the end of this panel is placed near the wood heater, where it is used often to split kindling for woodstove fires. A small pile of wood scraps is tucked out of the way beneath the radial arm saw. Larger pieces of heater wood are conveniently stacked beneath cover outside the shop.

Figure 209. *A number of yard implements are within easy reach.* Photo by Michael Eckerman

A 10-inch radial arm saw for cutting pieces of lumber of varying length is the only woodworking power tool used in our shop. With many years of use, we have found this saw to be more accurate, easier, and safer to use than any other type of power saw. For instance, the blade of this saw turns above one's work, and except when ripping, the material being sawn remains stationary while the blade is accurately and safely pulled across and through the wood. We also use the radial arm saw in preference to using a table saw because long boards are more easily cut or ripped with this tool. (The front access door of our shop swings open to align bench B7 with bench B6, thus extending bench support in order to cut long boards.) The many convenient adjustments that may be made with a radial arm saw give it great flexibility in use. The arm may be raised or lowered to adjust to a specific depth of cut or it can be swung left or right and locked in position for various angle cuts. Motor and blade tilt to make various angles for mitered cuts. Thus, by swinging the arm or by tilting the blade, compound mitered cuts are possible.

Adjacent to the right of the radial arm saw is a panel (W13) on which are hung all of the shop's saw blades used to cut metal, masonry, and various kinds of wood (Fig. 211, position ⚠10). Since this part of the project area is assigned for wood cutting, we have provided space on this panel for the three most essential wood guiding tools; the carpenter's square, sliding T-bevel, and combination square. Above the saw blades is found our collection of handsaws, including three crosscut saws, 5, 8, and 12 point; coping saw; backsaw; ripsaw; compass saw; and nail saw. On a shelf, directly beneath the saws, we store extra handles, a saw set, and a handsaw sharpener. This last item is a triangular file holder which has a built-in gauge with which to accurately set both the pitch and angle of saw teeth.

Figure 210. *Tools used to cut firewood and repair fencing hang in another area.* Photo by Michael Eckerman

Figure 211. *A panel containing all of the shop's saw blades used to cut metal, masonry, and wood.* Photo by Michael Eckerman

Figure 212. *A quiet corner of the woodworking wing reserved for desk work and storing paint supplies.* Photo by Michael Eckerman

Chapter 22
WOODWORKING AND SUPPLIES

A corner of the woodworking wing of our shop (Fig. 212), that receiving the least air-borne dust and flying sawdust, is reserved for paint supplies and painting activity. Cabinet C4 provides storage for gallon and quart containers of paint, while lower shelf BS3 holds larger 5-gallon containers of commonly used materials, like creosote, linseed oil, and paint thinner, which are always purchased in bulk quantity. In addition, we mix our own wood stains in 5-gallon amounts. See *The Owner-Built Pole Frame House* (Charles Scribner's Sons, 1981), page 112, for the formula used. All paint mixing and small-items painting is done on a 6-foot-long counter (B4). On the wall (W9) above this counter hangs a large assortment of brushes and other painting paraphernalia, such as putty knives, a utility knife, scrapers, wire brushes, and paint rollers. The shelf above the paint counter (TS4) contains paint-related supplies, like sandpaper, white glue, construction mastic cartridges and applicator gun, caulking cartridges, spackling compound, muriatic acid, etc. Here on this shelf, we also store a 1-gallon container of oil-and-gas mixture for two-cycle engines.

In Figure 212, position A you will notice a 30-inch-wide cabinet (C5), mounted on the wall between the paint bench (B4) and the woodworking bench (B5), that has a door which hinges downward to form a desk top. Inside this cabinet, an ample shelf carries the large volumes of shop and repair manuals for all of the equipment used on the homestead, including metal and woodworking references. On another shelf are a few basic drawing supplies—graph paper, scales, compass, pencils, T-square, triangles, and a protractor—with which to prepare the elementary working drawings necessary to build complex projects.

Atop this desk cabinet rest our two chain saws, and on the shelf immediately below are found parts for chain saws and other two-cycle engines: spare chains, plugs, files, etc. On the shelf below the desk top, clean shop rags are stored.

Similar to the vise used in the metalworking section of the shop, the vise of the woodworking section is located centrally, in proximity to all workbench activity. On the wall (W10) above the bench, racks are mounted that hold the following commonly used woodworking hand tools:

- screwdriver sets
- awl
- push drill
- rasp-file rack
- auger bits (No. 4 to 16 and ⅞ inch to 3 inch expansion bit)
- 12-inch ratchet brace
- hand drill
- ¾-inch box tape
- 16 oz. curved claw hammer

139

Drawers below the bench hold seldom-used hand tools. On the far left (D8), all tools related to masonry work, like trowels, are kept. In drawer D7, one finds measuring and marking tools, such as the chalk box, nylon line, line level, plumb bob, and a 50-foot steel tape. Tools with cutting edges that require special protection are placed in a drawer immediately to the right of the wood vise. In this drawer (D6) are the jack, smoothing, and block planes; 10-inch drawknife; butt, pocket, and mill chisel sets—¼ inch, ½ inch, 1 inch; and a 3½ inch half hatchet. The remaining drawer contains miscellaneous hand tools, like the staple gun, pliers, hacksaw, punch sets, and duplicate items.

Opposite the workbench, on wall panel W12, we store those rarely used tools that are too cumbersome to store elsewhere. These include a 6-foot straightedge, 24-inch goosenecked wrecking bar, 24-inch carpenter's level, and a four-piece set of adjustable clamps. Various types and sizes of nails are found in containers or bins lining the shelves of the cabinet (C7), directly below this panel. Bins for large quantities and 2-pound coffee can containers are used—a total of eighteen separate spaces for nails. The bins contain 2d, 4d, 8d, 10d, 16d, 20d, and 40d common nails, while cans contain the following: 4d, 8d casing nails; 4d, 6d, and 8d spiral-threaded shank nails; 1-inch concrete nails; 4d and 8d galvanized nails; brads; ¾-inch and 1½-inch roofing nails; 4d, 6d, and 8d annular-threaded shank nails—a total of eleven kinds of nails. A shallow bin extending the full length of this panel is storage for used (bent or rusty) and odd-sized nails. It is amazing how often we are drawn to this particular receptacle, seeking a nail not commonly stocked for a special function or needing a quantity of large nails with which to fasten wooden members to concrete—as when large, odd nails were driven into anchor blocks and door jambs to secure them to the masonry walls of our shop when they were built.

A wall cabinet at C6 stores numerous hardward items needed for the homestead. Hinges are in constant use for gates, doors, and cabinets. Also in frequent use are catches, knobs and pulls, casters, locks, brackets, handles, hasps, and metal braces, like the T-plate, corner brace, corner iron and mending plates. Next to this cabinet, supported by hooks, a 6-foot stepladder hangs on the wall at W11.

Chapter 23
CONCLUSION

Below the woodworking bench on shelf BS4 are stored the portable power tools we accumulated through the years when speed was considered more important than skill, a time when proper use and maintenance of hand tools was a mystery to those of us working at shop crafts. It was also a time when a "finished" project was considered to be that high-gloss product typified by illustrations in popular shop magazines. Today, however, craftspeople are returning more and more to use of hand tools, just as we have chosen to do in our shopwork. Thus, our power tools occupy a relatively inaccessible storage place, awaiting the time when they will be replaced entirely with our skill and confidence in using hand tools.

Rather than strive for precise, highly finished products, we seek to make useful articles that are simple, clean, and functional. Embellishments can wait for a rainy day. We prefer, instead, the eminently workable-but-funky over items or work that is craftsmanship-perfect. Shop production has too long been influenced by the superficial requirements of semi-professional specialty artisans. Those who wish to spend their lives refining their work may insist upon such high standards of proficiency. We, however, prefer to cultivate amateur status—a useful working knowledge of the general principles of shop practice, from automotive mechanics to plumbing, electrical, welding, furniture making, etc. Shopwork is but one aspect of homesteading, more for maintenance

and repair of homestead articles and implements than for building finely finished artifacts.

Our power tools became obsolete when we mastered the use of hand tools. A primary objection to the use of power tools, aside from their noise and hazard, is that they limit close contact between the maker, the tool, and the material. Part of the reason for a shop like ours is to experience the *process* of creation as well as the joy of producing useful things for homestead living. When a workshop-made product is used on the homestead, its value endures long after its creation.

A case in point—a fitting terminus to this book—is the following recital of the process we experienced when we built an important tool, one used daily everywhere about our homestead. This device, a sturdy two-wheeled cart (Fig. 213), was originally envisioned by us as useful for transporting shop tools to on-site projects around our homestead. Once it was built, we also found it especially useful for hauling firewood from our woodlot and bringing mulching material from the pasture to the barn. The design of the original two-wheeled utility garden cart is attributed to Thomas Jefferson, who, while observing work performance at Monticello, discovered that starting to push and stopping a wheelbarrow were the most energy-consuming aspects of its use. He also found that substantial effort was required just to keep its load balanced.

Figure 214.

Figure 213. *Our sturdy two-wheel cart designed originally for transporting shop tools to on-site projects . . .*

Copying Jefferson's model, contemporary cart manufacturers have used strong, light-weight bicycle wheels on their carts. But close inspection of these carts reveals flimsy framework for their unreasonable cost. We therefore found ways to structurally and functionally improve this design.

A homestead utility garden cart has three components: wheels, frame, and container. (Essentially, all cart wheels are manufactured by a single company, the Sun Wheel Company of Idaho. We had no difficulty arranging with this manufacturer to distribute these wheels to interested readers who intend to build their own cart. Please write to us for particulars.) The iron framework, heated and bent, is made of used

Figure 215.

Figure 216.
. . . that became indispensable for other homestead chores.

sucker rod sold by the pound at any metal salvage yard. A few welds are made (see Figure 217). The container is a discarded animal kennel, used by airline companies on a one-way-only basis to transport pets on airplanes (Fig. 218).

In a few hours', time, we had built ourselves a functioning cart that cost us (including high shipping charges) one-tenth of any commercial product on the market. Furthermore, our cart is more versatile, better designed, and more sturdily constructed than its factory-built counterpart.

This, in short, is an instance in which the homestead workshop was put to good use. We saved money and achieved a more useful, better-built product. With years of use and practice, such opportunities multiply for shopworkers, adding to their personal joy and satisfaction from participation in the work process. The homestead workshop makes experiences such as these attainable in a very real, enduring sense.

Note: We would very much like to make contact with homesteaders who wish to use or have used our workshop building plans and/or layouts.

Barbara and Ken Kern
PO Box 817
North Fork, CA 93643

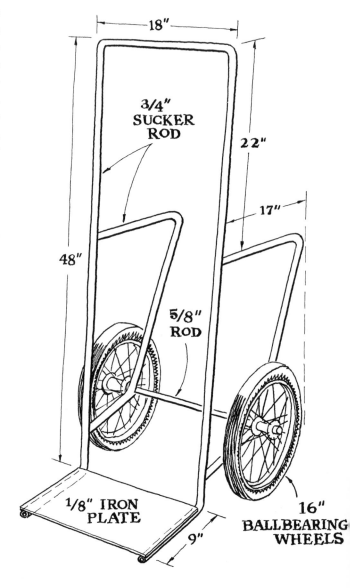

Figure 217. *Dimensions for our homestead cart.*

Figure 218. *By attaching a discarded pet carrier, the cart becomes an enclosed transportable container.*

TABLES

1. DECIMAL EQUIVALENTS

	1/64—	.016
1/32—		.031
	3/64—	.047
1/16—		.0625
	5/64—	.078
3/32—		.094
	7/64—	.109
1/8—		.125
	9/64—	.141
5/32—		.156
	11/64—	.172
3/16—		.1875
	13/64—	.203
7/32—		.219
	15/64—	.234
1/4—		.250
	17/64—	.266
9/32—		.281
	19/64—	.297
5/16—		.3125
	21/64—	.328
11/32—		.344
	23/64—	.359
3/8—		.375
	25/64—	.391
13/32—		.406
	27/64—	.422
7/16—		.4375
	29/64—	.453
15/32—		.469
	31/64—	.484
1/2—		.500
	33/64—	.516
17/32—		.531
	35/64—	.547
9/16—		.5625
	37/64—	.578
19/32—		.594
	39/64—	.609
5/8—		.625
	41/64—	.641
21/32—		.656
	43/64—	.672
11/16—		.6875
	45/64—	.703
23/32—		.719
	47/64—	.734
3/4—		.750
	49/64—	.766
25/32—		.781
	51/64—	.797
13/16—		.8125
	53/64—	.828
27/32—		.844
	55/64—	.859
7/8—		.875
	57/64—	.891
29/32—		.906
	59/64—	.922
15/16—		.9375
	61/64—	.953
31/32—		.969
	63/64—	.984
1—		1.000

2. DRILL SPEEDS

Diameter of Drill	Brass Bronze	Castiron Mild Steel
INCHES	RPM	RPM
1/16	9170	1833
1/8	4585	917
3/16	3056	611
1/4	2287	458
5/16	1830	367
3/8	1525	306
7/16	1307	262
1/2	1143	229
5/8	915	183
3/4	762	153
7/8	654	131
1	571	115

3. TAP DRILL SIZES

Size of Thread	National Coarse			National Fine		
	Threads Per Inch	Tap Drill Size*	Decimal Equivalent of Tap Drill	Threads Per Inch	Tap Drill Size*	Decimal Equivalent of Tap Drill
0	. . . .	. . . . . .	. . . .	80	3/64	.0469
1	64	53	.0595	72	53	.0595
2	56	50	.0700	64	50	.0700
3	48	47	.0785	56	45	.0820
4	40	43	.0890	48	42 (3/32)	.0935
5	40	38	.1015	44	37 (7/64)	.1040
6	32	36	.1065	40	33	.1130
8	32	29	.1360	36	29	.1360
10	24	25	.1495	32	21 (5/32)	.1590
12	24	16	.1770	28	14 (3/16)	.1820
1/4	20	7 (13/64)	.2010	28	3 (7/32)	.2130
5/16	18	F (1/4)	.2570	24	I (17/64)	.2720
3/8	16	5/16	.3125	24	Q (21/64)	.3320
7/16	14	U (23/64)	.3680	20	25/64	.3906
1/2	13	27/64	.4219	20	29/64	.4531
9/16	12	31/64	.4844	18	33/64	.5156
5/8	11	17/32	.5312	18	37/64	.5781
3/4	10	21/32	.6562	16	11/16	.6875
7/8	9	49/64	.7656	14	13/16	.8125
1	8	7/8	.8750	14	15/16	.9375

*To produce approximately 75 percent full thread

4. TIP SIZES AND PRESSURES FOR OXYACETYLENE WORK

WELDING

Tip Size	Drill Size for Tip	Pressure in Pounds		Thickness of Metal
		Acetylene	Oxygen	
0	71	1	1	Up to 1/32″
1	63	1	1	Up to 1/16″
2	58	2	2	1/16″ to 1/8″
3	54	3	3	1/8″ to 3/16″
4	52	4	4	3/16″ to 1/4″
5	48	5	5	1/4″ to 3/8″
6	44	6	6	3/8″ to 1/2″
7	40	7	7	1/2″ to 5/8″
8	36	8	8	5/8″ to 1″
9	32	9	9	1″ and over

CUTTING

Tip Size	Pressure in Pounds		Maximum Cutting Range
	Acetylene	Oxygen	
0–4	3	8–12	Up to 1/8″
1–4	3½	10–15	Up to 1/4″
2–4	4	15–20	1/4″ to 1/2″
3–4	5	20–25	1/2″ to 3/4″
4–4	6	25–30	3/4″ to 1″
5–4	7	30–40	1″ to 2″

GLOSSARY OF TOOLS AND SHOP TERMS

It will probably take years for the average homesteader to put together a fully equipped workshop, for even those tools and materials that are essential to the maintenance of homestead life take time to learn to use as well as to acquire. Actually, the skill to use tools tends to be gained at a pace slower than that by which money to purchase them is acquired. Accordingly, with the following symbols we have noted which tools are basic to shop operation (***), which are handy but expensive and therefore purchasable at a later time (**), and which are seldom needed and better borrowed or rented (*). A torque wrench, for instance, falls into this latter designation: it may be used but once or twice a year, mainly when replacing an engine head. A socket set, on the other hand, is used often and is worth saving for. The adjustable (crescent) wrench is a basic, indispensable tool. If the tool listed is not preceded by one of these symbols, it is included here merely to acquaint the reader with the full range of tools in current use in homestead workshops across the country.

We believe the serious shopworker should also acquire a vocabulary descriptive of shop tools, materials, and processes. Use of appropriate terminology may one day save you considerable time and money. Costly delays and errors may be avoided when, for example, you are able to properly order supplies appropriate to an urgently needed project. Therefore, in this glossary we include those terms that should be familiar to anyone working with mechanical and woodworking tools and processes.

abrasion The process of reducing material by grinding instead of cutting.

abrasive Grinding material such as sandstone, emery, or carborundum.

a.c. Alternating current. An electric current that alternates or reverses in direction at rapid regular intervals, usually 120 times per second.

acetylene gas An illuminating gas (C_2H_2) resulting from the action of water on calcium carbide. Used for oxyacetylene welding.

adapter A device by means of which objects of different sizes are made interchangeable.

*__adjustable clamps__ Clamps for temporarily holding wide objects.

***__adjustable wrench__ A single tool designed to turn nuts of various sizes.

adz A cutting tool with the blade set at right angles to the handle. Used for rough-dressing timber.

Allen screws Cap screws and setscrews having hexagonal sockets in the head adjusted by means of a hexagonal key.

allowance The minimum clearance or

maximum interference intentionally permitted between mating parts.

alloy A homogeneous combination of two or more metals.

American screw gauge A standard gauge for checking the diameter of wood screws and machine screws.

American Standard Pipe Threads The thread used on wrought iron or steel steam, gas, and water pipes.

angle divider A tool for bisecting angles.

angle iron A strip of structural iron, the section of which is in the form of a right angle.

anneal To heat metal to a critical temperature and cool slowly in order to soften it, reduce brittleness, and make it more workable.

anvil A steel or iron block upon which forging is done.

arc welding The process of joining two pieces of metal using a carbon-arc flame. The piece to be welded is usually made the positive terminal, the welding rod the negative. The work is touched with the rod and withdrawn slightly, causing an arc.

assemble To collect or put in place the parts of a machine or other manufactured article.

auger A wood-boring tool of large size with a handle at right angles to the tool line.

***auger bit** An auger without a handle, to be used in a brace. *See* brace.

***auger bit file** A specially designed file for sharpening auger bits.

***aviation snips** Hand shears with lever advantage for cutting sheet metal.

***awl** A small pointed tool for making holes for nails or screws.

back off To remove metal behind the cutting edge to relieve friction in cutting, as in taps.

back out To run back a tap or die after a thread has been cut.

*backsaw** A saw having a metal rim on the back to stiffen the blade. Used commonly with a miter box.

ball bearing A bearing in which freely rolling metal balls turn in a socket round the shaft, thus reducing friction.

ball-peen hammer The type of hammer commonly used by machinists. One end of the head is rounded or ball shaped for riveting or peening; the surface of the other end is flat and is used for striking a chisel.

*bar clamp** A clamp consisting of a long bar and two clamping jaws, used by woodworkers for clamping large work.

bastard file A medium file, neither coarse nor fine.

bead A weld line.

bearing The support or carrier for a rotating shaft.

***bench** A strong table equipped with vise and other implements to facilitate the work performed on it.

*bench hook** A flat piece of wood with cleats on both sides, one at each end, used to prevent injury to the bench top during certain operations.

***bench plane** Plane kept on the bench, in constant use, e.g. jack and smoothing planes.

benchwork Term used to distinguish work carried on at the bench or vise from machine work.

*Bernard plier** A lever-advantage plier having parallel grips.

bevel A tool used for testing the accuracy of work cut to an angle or bevel.

*bevel protractor** An adjustable tool for measuring angles.

***bit brace** A device for holding bits, so constructed that good leverage is had for the turning thereof.

bit stop A device attached to a bit to control the drilling or boring to a desired depth.

blacksmith A smith who forges metal by hand.

blade The flat, active working part of a

tool, instrument, or device, as the blade of a knife.

***block plane   A small plane used chiefly in working end grain.

*block and tackle   One or more sheaves or pulley blocks and the rope, chain, or cable used in connection with them.

blowtorch   A portable device for securing intense local heat, using gasoline for fuel. Used by plumbers.

bolt   A fastening; commonly a piece of metal with a head and threaded body for the reception of a nut.

bolt cutter   Hand-operated shears for cutting bolts, links of chain, etc.

bore   The internal diameter of a pipe, cylinder, or hole for shafting.

boring   Making or finishing circular holes in wood or metal.

**bow saw   A saw with a thin, narrow blade held in tension by the leverage obtained through a turnbuckle.

brace   A holder for drill bits.

brazing   Joining two or more pieces of metal with an alloy.

***breast drill   A small mechanism used in the drilling of holes in metal by hand.

broad ax   An ax with a broad blade, used for cutting timber.

buffing wheels   Polishing wheels made of many disks of cotton or wool cloth which serve to carry abrasive powders, rouge, etc.

burr   The ragged or turned-down edge of a piece of metal resulting from grinding, cutting, or punching.

*burring reamer   A tapered reamer used for countersinking and for removing burrs caused in cutting pipe.

bushing   A sleeve or liner for a bearing, which permits accurate adjustment and inexpensive repair.

butt hinge   A hinge secured to the edge of a door and the face of the jamb which butts against the edge of the door when it is shut, as distinguished from a strap hinge.

butt welding   A weld in which the two pieces to be connected do not overlap but are welded directly at their ends.

**C clamp   A frequently used form of clamp shaped like the letter C; pressure is obtained by means of a thumbscrew.

*caliper   A tool principally for measuring the diameter of circular work.

caliper rule   A graduated scale, with a fixed head, which slides in a groove in a second piece. Used for both inside and outside calipering.

cant hook   Consists of a stout wooden pole with a hinged steel hook attached near one end. Used for rolling logs. Also called a peavy.

cap screw   A finished machine bolt used either with or without a nut.

carbon arc torch   A weld made by melting metal rod between carbon and the metal to be welded.

Carborundum   A trade name covering silicon carbide and other abrasive products.

***carpenter's level   A bubble level mounted in a metal or wooden beam used in leveling vertical or horizontal surfaces.

carriage bolt   An oval or buttonhead black bolt with a square neck which prevents the bolt from turning while the nut is being tightened.

case hardening   The process by which a thin, hard film is formed on the surface of iron-base alloys.

castellated   Formed like a castle, as a castellated nut, which has a portion of its length turned and slotted for the reception of cotter pins.

cast iron   Iron of ordinary use, cast in molds; has high carbon content, cannot be rolled, forged, or tempered.

caulking   Making a joint tight or leakproof by forcing plastic material between parts that are not tightly fitted.

**center punch   A steel punch with one end ground to a point; used for laying out work in metal.

*chain hoist   A block and tackle in which chain is used instead of rope.

chain pipe vise A portable vise utilizing a heavy chain to fasten the pipe in the jaw.

*****chalk box** Contains a reel of line and chalk dust for marking straight lines on work.

*****chalk line** Used frequently for making a straight line. When raised and allowed to snap back, a straight chalk line is made. Also called snap line.

chamfer A beveled edge or cut-off corner.

channel iron Rolled bars consisting of a web and two flanges.

chasing threads The process of cutting threads with a chaser, which usually is a flat tool containing several teeth of the desired pitch.

check valve A valve that automatically closes to prevent the backflow of water.

*****chisel** A tool that comes in a great variety of shapes, whose cutting principle is that of the wedge.

circular saw A saw whose teeth are spaced around the edge of a circular disk running upon a central arbor.

***clamp** A tool for holding portions of work together, both in wood and metal.

*****claw hammer** A hammer with a face for driving nails and a claw for use as a nail puller.

clinch To secure firmly, as by bending down the ends of protruding nails.

close nipple Twice as long as standard pipe thread, with no shoulder between the two sets of threads.

*****cold chisel** An all-steel chisel, without handle, used for chipping metals.

cold-rolled steel Marketed with a bright, smooth surface and made quite accurate to size so that for many purposes no machining is necessary.

combination pliers Pliers adjustable for the size of opening by means of a slip joint.

*****combination square** A square containing a bevel protractor, level, and center head in addition to a movable square head.

****come-along** A ratchet-type hand winch.

compass plane A plane used for smoothing concave surfaces.

****compass saw** A type of handsaw with a small tapering blade, used for cutting in a small circle.

compression spring A helical spring designed to operate under pressure, therefore tending to shorten when in action.

***coping saw** Consists of a narrow blade carried on pins set in a steel bow frame. Used for cutting curves.

cotter pin A form of split pin which is inserted into a hole near the end of a bolt to prevent a nut from working loose.

countersink To recess a hole conically for the head of a screw or rivet.

coupling A fitting with inside threads only, used for connecting two pieces of pipe.

*****crosscut saw** A saw for cutting wood across the grain. The action of its teeth is similar to that of a knife.

cross grain A section of wood taken at right angles, or at a low angle, with the direction of the longitudinal fiber.

cross-peen hammer A hammer with a wedge-shaped peening edge at right angles to the direction of the handle.

*****crowbar** A heavy pinch bar of round iron or steel flattened to a chisel-like point at one end. Used as a lever.

cup grease A heavy-bodied, semisolid grease used as a lubricant.

*****curved-claw hammer** A hammer with a claw curved back toward the handle. Used for general work.

***curved-tooth file** File teeth made in a curved contour across the file. Used for filing soft material.

cut of file The manner in which the face of a file is cut, and from which a file takes its name, such as smooth cut, rough cut, bastard, etc.

cutting oils Any of the heavy oils or combination of oils used as a metal lubricant in machining operations.

****cutting pliers** Pliers which, in addition to the flat jaws, have a pair of nippers placed to one side for cutting off wire.

d.c.   Direct current. An electric current that flows in one direction.

dado   A groove cut out across the edge or face of a board to receive another member.

dead-smooth file   The finest-cut file made.

decimal equivalent   The value of a fraction expressed as a decimal.

depth gauge   A gauge used by wood- and metal-workers for testing the depth of holes and recessed portions.

***die**   An internal screw used for cutting an outside thread.

***die stock**   A lever or wrench used in operating threading dies by hand.

dinging hammer   A hand hammer used for removing dents and bends from sheet metal.

***dividers**   Compasses for measuring or setting off distances.

dog   A small piece of metal with two or more points for binding pieces of wood together while they are being worked.

****double-bitted axe**   An axe having a cutting edge on both sides.

double-cut   Refers to a double-cut file, one with two rows of teeth crossing each other.

dovetail   An interlocking joint. A tenon shaped like a dove's tail fits into a similarly shaped mortise.

dowel   A wood or metal pin used in making permanent joints.

draw filing   A metal-polishing operation, with a single-cut file, to remove finish marks from the face or edges of a metal object.

drawing of temper   The heating of steel to red heat and allowing it to cool slowly. The reverse of hardening or tempering.

****drawknife**   A two-handled wood-cutting tool having a long, narrow blade, the handles being at right angles to the blade.

dress   To restore a tool to its original shape and sharpness by forging or grinding.

drift pin   A round tapered pin driven into rivet holes to bring them into perfect alignment.

drill   A tool for boring holes in metal or wood.

*****drill bit**   A rotating tool for cutting holes in solid material.

***drill gauge**   A flat steel plate drilled with holes of different sizes, marked so that the size of a drill bit can be easily determined by fitting it to the plate.

***drill-grinding gauge**   Used for checking the length and angle of the cutting lips of the drill.

****drill press**   A geared machine tool used for drilling holes in metal.

***drill-press vise**   A special vise used on the table of a drill press to hold the parts being drilled.

drive home   The setting of a part into its final position by the action of blows, as from a hammer.

drive screw   A type of screw intended to be set by blows of a hammer but which can be removed with a screwdriver.

drop forging   One formed in dies under a drop hammer.

edged tools   Cutting tools used in the handicrafts, especially in woodworking.

elbow   A fitting joining two pipes at an angle.

****electric drill**   Refers to the electrically operated, self-contained hand drill.

electrode   The part or parts of a resistance welding machine through which the welding current and pressure are applied directly to the work.

emery cloth   Powdered emery glued onto thin cloth. Used for removing file marks and polishing metallic surfaces.

emery wheel   A high-speed grinding wheel made of emery.

****expansion bit**   A boring bit having a cutter or cutters arranged to permit radial adjustments, to enable one tool to bore holes of different diameters.

expansion bolt   A bolt equipped with a split casing that acts as a wedge. Used for attaching whatever is desired to brick or concrete.

extension bit A bit with an extra-long shank to permit the drilling of deep holes or used where obstructions would make impossible the use of a regular bit.

*****extension cord** A length of cable or lamp cord fitted with a plug and socket to bring light or power closer to the point where it is needed.

eyebolt A bolt provided with a hole or eye at one end, instead of the usual head.

fabricating The act of building or putting together.

fastening devices Such holding implements as bolts, screws, and keys.

fatigue of material Material that has been long subjected to severe or even just moderate straining deteriorates in strength and will break under loads previously sustained with safety.

***feeler** Gauge for determining the size of a piece of work, the accuracy of the test depending on one's sense of touch.

female The recessed portion of any piece of work into which another part fits.

fence An adjustable metal bar or strip mounted on the table of a circular saw to act as a guide and ensure a parallel cut.

****fence pliers** A combination hammer, wire cutter, and gripper.

***fence stretcher** A ratchet-type hand winch.

ferrule Ring of metal enclosing and confining the wood around the tang of an edged tool to prevent splitting.

*****file** A hard steel instrument, made in various shapes and sizes, for smoothing wood or metal.

****file card** A kind of brush fitted with short, fine wires. Used for cleaning files.

file hard When a metal is so hard that it cannot be filed it is said to be "file hard."

fillister plane A kind of plane used for grooving timber or for cutting rabbets.

***firmer chisel** A chisel commonly used on the workbench.

firmer tools The ordinary short chisels and gouges of woodworkers. Used in benchwork.

***flaring tool** A tool for widening the mouth of copper tubing before it is joined to another piece.

flexible shaft A shaft made of jointed links encased in flexible tubing. Used to transmit power in places where a straight shaft could not be used.

*****flex tape** Retractable metal measuring rule wound inside a metal case.

flush Parts are said to be flush when their surfaces are on the same level.

flux Any substance or mixture used to promote the fusion of metals.

folding rule A collapsible instrument used for measuring.

***fore plane** A plane intermediate in size between a jack and a jointer plane.

forge To form a piece of metal by hammering it while it is hot.

****framing chisel** Used for framing and other rough carpentry tasks.

friction tape An impregnated-cotton insulating tape used to cover the rubber tape required to protect a splice in electrical conductors.

galvanize To coat iron with zinc by dipping the iron into molten zinc.

garnet paper Paper coated with garnet grains. Used in the same manner as sandpaper.

gasket Paper, metal, rubber, or other especially prepared material used to prevent leaking.

gauge An instrument or device for determining the size of parts. Gauges for different purposes are known by specific names.

gear ratio The relation between the number of teeth on driving and driven gears.

***gimlet** A small wood-boring tool with a handle attached at right angles to the bit.

glass cutter Any device used for cutting glass to size; usually a diamond or a small rotary wheel set in a handle.

*****goggles** Shrouded dark glasses worn by welders and grinders as a protection against eye injury.

*gouge   A cutting chisel that has either a concave or a convex cutting surface.

**grease gun   A device for forcing lubricant into a bearing.

grind   To sharpen, to reduce to size, or to remove material by contact with a rotating abrasive wheel.

**grinder   A tool for removing metal by abrasion.

***grindstone   Stone against which tools and materials are abraded by grinding. Grindstones are natural sandstone.

grit   The particles used to make up grinding wheels. The size of these particles is referred to by a grit number.

gusset   An angle bracket or brace used to stiffen a corner or angular portion of a piece of work.

***hacksaw   A light-framed saw used for cutting metal, operated by power or by hand.

hammer   An instrument or tool used for striking blows in metalworking, driving nails, etc.

***hand drill   A drilling machine operated by hand.

hand file   A file with parallel sides but tapered in thickness. It is double-cut, with various degrees of fineness. Its principal use is in finishing flat surfaces.

***handsaw   An ordinary one-handled saw, either rip or cross-cut, used by woodworkers.

hand vise   A small vise held in the hand. Used for clamping small, light work.

hanger bolt   Consists of a lag screw at one end and a machine-bolt thread and nut at the other. Used for attaching hangers to woodwork.

hardening   Heating and quenching to produce increased hardness.

hasp   A fastening, as for a door, usually passing over a staple and secured by a padlock.

hex head   A common shop expression referring to screws and bolts with hexagonal heads.

high-carbon steel   A rather general term applied to steels with good tempering qualities that are suitable for cutting tools.

hold-down clamp   A clamp mounted on a surface, such as that of a workbench, for holding work in place.

**hone or oilstone   A stone used for whetting edged tools, to give the clean, fine edge necessary for clean cutting.

hydraulic jack   A lifting jack, actuated by a small force pump enclosed within it and operated by a lever from the outside.

*hydrometer   An instrument for determining the specific gravity of liquids.

I beam   A steel beam shaped like the letter I. Used in structural work.

idle wheel or idler   A gear transmitting motion between two active gears, or a pulley used against a belt to take up slack.

*inside calipers   A calipers with the points at the end of the legs turned outward instead of inward, so that it may be used for gauging inside diameters.

jack   A mechanical device used for lifting heavy loads through short distances with a minimal expenditure of manual power.

***jack plane   A plane used for roughing off or bringing the wood down to approximate size.

jig   A device to hold and locate a piece of work and guide the tools that operate upon it.

joinery   A term relating to the various types of joints used by woodworkers.

*jointer plane   An iron plane used for all kinds of plane work.

journal   That part of a shaft or spindle that rotates in a bearing.

kerf   The cut made by a saw.

key   A wedge-shaped strip of iron or steel used for preventing wheels from slipping around upon their axles.

*keyhole saw   A small, tapered-blade saw used for cutting keyholes.

keyway   A groove in which a key is placed

for the purpose of binding something, as a crank, gear, or pulley, on a shaft.

knurl To finish by roughing or milling a surface to permit a better grip.

lag screw A square-headed, heavy wood screw.

lap weld A weld made on the overlapped edges of plates, maintaining an even thickness of material.

layout Planning, or marking out to full size, the development or pattern for shopwork.

left-hand thread A screw thread so cut that the bolt, screw, or nut has to be turned in a counterclockwise motion to engage or tighten it.

leg vise A bench vise with a leg or strut reaching to the floor.

***level** A tool for testing with regard to the horizontal.

*****line level** A bubble level designed to hook onto a string. Used in leveling a string line.

lip In machine-shop practice, the cutting edge of a tool.

******locking C clamp** A device for temporarily holding parts together.

maintenance Proper care, repair, and keeping in good order.

male. The protruding portion of any piece of work that fits into another part.

malleable Capable of being hammered or rolled out without breaking or cracking.

*****mallet** A wooden hammer.

mandrel A shaft or spindle on which an object may be fixed for rotation.

marking gauge A woodworker's gauge used for scribing lines parallel to the edge of a board. It consists of a bar with an inserted pin or scribe and a sliding head, which may be adjusted by means of a thumbscrew.

micrometer caliper A caliper with a graduated screw attachment for measuring minute distances.

mild steel Low-carbon steel that welds but does not temper.

*****mill file** A single-cut file made in any cut from rough to dead-smooth.

millwork Finished woodwork, machined and partly assembled at the mill.

miter The joining of two pieces at an evenly divided angle, as the corner of a picture frame.

*****miter box** A device used as a guide in sawing miter joints.

miter cut A cut made at an angle of 45 degrees so that two pieces similarly cut will form a right angle when joined.

monkey wrench An adjustable wrench.

mortise A space hollowed out, as in a piece of wood, to receive a tenon; a mortise-and-tenon joint.

nail A slender piece of metal, one end of which is pointed, the other end having a head, either flattened or rounded. It is commonly used in fastening together several pieces of wood or other material by striking the head with a hammer.

*****nail puller** A mechanical device with two jaws, one of which has a heel, which provides leverage for gripping the nail and for pulling it from the wood.

*****nail set** A small rod of steel with one end drawn to a taper and slightly cupped to prevent it from slipping off the head of the nail. Used in sinking the head of a nail below the surface.

National Coarse thread, Fine thread Much used in automobile work; formerly known as S.A.E. thread; of the same form as U.S. Standard.

nest of saws A combination of compass saws consisting of several blades of different lengths for use in the same handle. Used for light work.

*****nippers** A pincerlike tool with sharp jaws for cutting.

nipple A short length of pipe threaded at both ends.

nonferrous metals Metals not containing iron.

nut   A small block of metal or other material commonly square or hexagonal in shape, having internal threads to receive a bolt.

O.D. pipe   Indicates outside diameter.

*offset screwdriver**   For tightening or removing screws in awkward positions. Heads are offset at right angles.

***oiler**   A small-size oil can.

oil hardening   The hardening of steel by quenching it in oil instead of water.

***oilstone**   A smooth stone used, when moistened with oil, for sharpening tools.

*outside caliper**   A caliper used for gauging outside measurements or sizes.

oxyacetylene   A mixture of oxygen and acetylene gas in such proportions as to produce the hottest flame known for practical use.

*paring chisel**   A long chisel used in making, paring, or slicing cuts, thus obtaining a smoother surface than would result if the cuts were taken directly across the grain.

peen   The small end of the head of a hammer, as the ball-peen hammer for metalworkers.

peening   Beating over or smoothing over a metallic surface with the peen end of a hammer.

Phillips machine screw   A metal- or wood-holding screw made in a variety of head forms and having a four-point star-shaped recess in the head that requires a special tool for setting.

pilot drill   A small drill used to start a hole in order to ensure a larger drill's running true to center.

pincers   A jointed instrument with two handles and a pair of grasping jaws for holding an object.

pinch bar   The shop name for crowbar.

pin punch   A long, slender punch used for driving out tight-fitting pins.

pipe compound   Material applied to pipe threads to prevent leaks.

pipe cutter   A tool for cutting wrought-iron pipes. The curved end that partly encircles the pipe carries one or more cutting disks. The feed of the cutter is regulated by a screw as the tool is rotated around the pipe.

pipe die   A screw plate used for cutting threads on pipe.

pipe fittings   Ells, tees, branch connectors, unions, etc. used in connecting pipes.

pipe thread   The V-type thread used on pipe and tubing, cut on a taper of 3/4 in. per foot, which ensures a thoroughly tight joint.

***pipe vise**   Pipe vises are of two kinds: the hinged-side type with V jaws for small pipes, and the chain type used for large pipes.

pitch   A term used to denote the number of threads per inch, or in gearing, to indicate the size of teeth.

play   The motion between poorly fitted or worn parts.

pliers   A pincerlike tool having broad, flat, roughened jaws.

plow plane   A grooving plane having an adjustable fence capable of being fitted with various irons for cutting grooves.

*plug tap**   The intermediate tap in a series of three: (1) starting tap, (2) plug tap, (3) bottoming tap.

plumb   To test or true up vertically, as a wall by means of a plumb line.

***plumb bob**   The weight used at the end of a plumb line.

pop rivet gun   For applying "blind," or accessible from single side rivets.

post drill   A drilling machine constructed for attachment to a post or column.

*prickpunch**   A small center punch. Also known as a layout punch.

propane torch   Heat source for soldering work.

*pry bar**   A lever, crowbar, etc.; any tool for raising or moving something by leverage.

puller Any mechanical or hydraulic device for removing, by pulling action, parts that are tightly fitted; e.g., a wheel puller or gear puller.

pulley A wheel used to transmit or receive power through a belt that travels over its face.

pulley block A sheave pulley or series of such pulleys, enclosed between metal or wooden side plates that carry the shaft or pin on which the pulleys revolve.

*****punch** A shearing tool made of steel, used to remove material whose shape is the same as that of the punch.

****push drill** A small drill used to bore holes in wood.

rabbet A rectangular groove or cut made in the edge of a board so that another, similarly cut, may fit into it to form a rabbet joint.

rabbet plane Used for planing into corners.

radial Extending outward from a center or axis.

****rasp** A filelike tool having coarse projections for abrasion.

rasp cut file A file tooth arrangement under which teeth are individually formed, one by one, by means of a narrow, punchlike chisel.

******ratchet bit brace** A bit brace with a ratchet attachment to permit operating in close quarters.

*****rattail file** Name commonly applied to round files.

****reamer** A tool with cutting edges, square or fluted, used for finishing drilled holes.

reducer Any one of the various pipe connections so constructed as to permit joining pipes of different sizes.

riffler A small rasp or file, usually curved, used for filing inside surfaces or for enlarging holes.

******ripsaw** An ordinary handsaw, used for sawing in the direction of the grain. Its teeth are so formed that the action is similar to that of a chisel.

rivet A short, metal, boltlike fastening, without threads, which is clinched by hammering.

*****rivet set** A steel punch with a hollow or cupped face. Used in the setting of rivets.

rough cut Usually the first or heavy cut taken in preparation for the finish cut.

roughing out To speedily remove excess material without regard to finish.

r.p.m. An abbreviation for revolutions per minute.

S.A.E. threads *See* National Coarse, Fine threads.

safe edge The uncut edge of a file that makes possible the protection of an adjacent surface when operating in a corner.

sandpaper Paper coated with sharp sand. Used as an abrasive, particularly for finishing surfaces of woodwork.

sawhorse A kind of rack on which wood is placed for sawing.

*****saw set** A tool for giving the proper "set" to the teeth of saws.

scraper A flat plate of steel used by woodworkers to smooth wood surfaces.

scrap iron A term covering all grades of salvaged iron or steel.

****scratch awl** A sharp-pointed piece of steel used for marking on metal.

screw box A tool for cutting wood threads.

******screwdriver** A bar or rod of steel with a handle at one end and flattened at the other to fit the slots in screwheads.

screw eye A wood screw with the head formed into a completely closed ring or circle.

screw, machine A screw with a solid head slotted so that it can be turned with a screwdriver.

****scribe awl or scriber** A pointed steel instrument for making fine lines on wood or metal for layout work.

second cut Indicates the spacing of teeth on a file. Second cut indicates a degree of roughness between bastard and smooth and may be either single or double cut.

second tap   A tap with a few end threads tapered to follow the first or taper tap.

setscrew   A plain screw having a square or other shaped head, used for tightening purposes and for locking adjustable parts in position.

shackle   A connecting link or device for fastening parts together, usually in such a manner as to permit some motion.

shaft   An axle or bar, usually cylindrical, used to support rotating pieces or transmit power or motion by rotation.

shank   That part of a tool which fits into the tool holder.

**shears   A tool with two blades, for cutting metals.

sheet-metal screw   Self-tapping screw with threads along the full length of the shaft.

shim   A thin strip of metal placed between adjacent surfaces to allow adjustment for fit.

single-cut file   A file having parallel lines of teeth running diagonally across its face in one direction only.

slack   Loose; that looseness of parts that must be removed before applied power becomes effective.

*sledge   A long-handled heavy hammer used with both hands.

sleeve   A hollow tube or cylinder that surrounds a rod or shaft.

slide caliper   A caliper with a slide graduated to show the movement of the measuring jaws.

*slip-joint pliers   Pliers that permit adjustment to a greater range of opening by a slipping motion of the two halves about the pin or rivet that connects them.

slip stone   A small wedge-shaped oilstone with rounded edges. It is held in the hand and used for whetting gouges.

*smoothing plane   A small plane.

snap rings   Hardened metal rings (broken circles) fixed in recessed parts to act as retainers.

snips   Another name for sheet-metal workers' hand shears.

socket chisel   The strongest kind of woodworker's chisel. The upper end of the shank terminates in a socket into which the handle is driven.

**socket wrench   Consists of a socket that fits over and completely encircles the nut or bolt head, a handle or lever (with or without a ratchet), and sometimes an extension to permit working in places not easily accessible.

solder   An alloy used for joining metals together under heat.

soldering copper   A tool, also called a soldering iron, used for applying heat to melt the solder and heat up the metals that are to be joined by soldering.

**smooth-cut file   A degree of file coarseness between second cut and dead-smooth.

***soap stone   Steatite, a soft talc in rock form, used for marking metal.

*soft-face hammer   A head made of soft metal or rawhide or plastic. Used on finished surfaces to avoid bruising them.

soldering iron   A copper point on a steel shank with a wooden handle. The point is applied to the solder laid on the joint to be fused.

***spirit level   An instrument for testing the horizontal and vertical accuracy of work. It consists of a glass tube or bulb nearly full of spirit and enclosed in a wood or metal case.

*splitting maul   A heavy hammer used for splitting cordwood.

spokeshave   A kind of double-handled plane for dressing curved woodwork.

*spring clamp   A device for temporarily holding fine parts together.

spot welding   A resistance-welding process wherein coalescence is produced by the heat obtained from resistance to the flow of electric current through the work parts held together under pressure by electrodes.

***square   An instrument having at least one right angle and two or more straight edges. Used to lay out or test the squareness of work.

**staple gun   A device to fasten by means of a staple.

*star drill A tool with a star-shaped point used for drilling in stone or masonry.

***steel square The ordinary steel try square used by machinists; also the large square used by carpenters.

steel wool Fine threads of steel matted together into a mass. Used principally for polishing or cleaning surfaces of wood or metal.

**Stillson wrench The pipe wrench of common use, named for its inventor, Henry Stillson.

*straight-claw hammer A hammer with its claw at right angles to the handle. Used for ripping.

***straightedge A bar of wood or metal with one edge true. Used for testing straight lines and surfaces.

**straight snips Hand shears for cutting sheet metal.

stud bolt A bolt threaded at both ends, with a blank space between to permit gripping with a pipe wrench.

sweat To coat with solder the surfaces to be joined, after which the surfaces are made to adhere by the application of heat.

***swivel vise A bench vise that may be rotated on its base to bring the work it holds into a better position.

*tackle The chain, rope, and pulleys, or blocks, used for hoisting purposes in the erection of heavy work.

**tap A fluted, threaded tool for cutting female or inside threads.

*tap and drill gauge Template for checking sizes.

taper A gradual and uniform decrease in size, as a tapered shaft.

**taper tap A tap with the threads at the end tapered considerably to make it easy to start in the hole.

**tap wrench The double-armed lever with which a tap is gripped and operated during the process of tapping holes.

template Any temporary pattern, guide, or model by which work is either marked out or by which its accuracy is checked.

tenon A tongue projecting from the end of a piece of timber which, with the mortise into which it fits, constitutes a mortise-and-tenon joint.

tension spring Any spring designed to be operated under a pulling strain.

*thickness gauge or feeler Shaped somewhat like a pocketknife, with blades varying in thickness by thousandths of an inch.

threaded rod Rod threaded its full length.

threads per inch Refers to thread size.

*three-cornered file A file whose cross-section is triangular.

three-square file A term commonly applied to a three-cornered file. Used for saw sharpening.

thumb nut A wing nut or one so shaped that it can be operated by thumb and forefinger.

thumbscrew A screw to be turned with the thumb and finger.

***tin snips The ordinary hand shears used by sheet-metal workers.

tip cleaner For cleaning openings of an oxyacetylene torch.

toenailing The driving of nails slantwise, as in floor laying, to avoid having nailheads show on the surface.

tolerance Allowable inexactness or error in the dimensions of manufactured machine parts.

T plate A metal plate shaped like a letter T used for strengthening a joint where the end of one and the side of another meet.

treadle That portion of a machine operated by the foot.

*try square A small square used by mechanics in testing the squareness of their work. Also used to lay off right angles.

tube punch A hand punch shaped somewhat like a pair of pliers and having a hollow tube or tubes for punching holes for snaps, eyelets, etc.

turnbuckle A form of coupling threaded to regulate tension in the rods it connects.

twist bits Similar to the twist drills used for drilling metal, but ground at a sharper angle. Used principally for boring holes for screws in wood.

***twist drill A drill made from round stock,

having two helical grooves extending through its effective length.

U bolt   A bolt shaped like the letter U and threaded at both ends.

universal joint   A type of coupling that permits the free rotation of two shafts whose axes are not in a straight line.

***utility knife**   A cutting knife with a single-edge blade held between the two sides of the knife.

V belt   A belt with a V section for use on grooved pulleys.

***vise**   A mechanical contrivance for holding a piece of wood or metal while it is being worked on.

***visegrip pliers**   Adjustable pliers that will clamp onto an object and stay.

warding file   A very thin, flat file used principally by locksmiths.

washer   A small, flat, perforated disk, used to secure the tightness of a joint, screw, etc.

web   A thin plate connecting two parts of a casting, forging, etc.

wedge   A piece of wood, or metal, V shaped in longitudinal section, used for producing strong pressure or for splitting a substance apart.

welding   Uniting of pieces of iron or steel by fusion accomplished by the oxyacetylene, electric, or hammering (forging) process.

*wheel dresser**   A tool for cleaning, resharpening, and truing the cutting faces of grinding wheels.

whetting   The "rubbing up" of a tool on an oilstone for the purpose of improving its cutting edge.

wing nut   A form of nut that is tightened or loosened by two thin flat wings extending from opposite sides; a thumb nut.

*wire gauge**   A gauge used for measuring the diameter of wire or the thickness of sheet metal.

wood chisel   A wood cutting tool.

wrecking bar   A steel bar with one end drawn to a thin edge, the other curved to a claw.

***wrench**   A tool for exerting a twisting strain, as in tightening a nut or bolt.

wrought iron   Iron that has had the major portion of its carbon, as well as the foreign elements that would effect its working value, removed.

INDEX